Revelations of Divine Love

Revelations of Divine Love

St. Julian, Anchoress of Norwich

TAN Books
Gastonia, North Carolina

This edition of *Revelations of Divine Love* is from the English translation by Grace Warrack, first published in 1901. It has been edited and transliterated by Fr. John Waiss, and was retypeset and republished by TAN Books in 2025.

Cover design by Caroline Green

Cover image: *A Dream* (oil on canvas) by Frederic Leighton. Public domain via Wikimedia Commons.

ISBN: 978-1-5051-3865-8
ePUB ISBN: 978-1-5051-3977-8

Published in the United States by
TAN Books
PO Box 269
Gastonia, NC 28053
www.TANBooks.com

Printed in the United States of America

Contents

Pope Benedict XVI on St. Julian

Dear Brothers and Sisters,

I still remember with great joy the Apostolic Journey I made in the United Kingdom last September. England is a land that has given birth to a great many distinguished figures who enhanced Church history with their testimony and their teaching. One of them, venerated both in the Catholic Church and in the Anglican Communion, is the mystic Julian of Norwich, of whom I wish to speak this morning.

The — very scant — information on her life in our possession comes mainly from her *Revelations of Divine Love in Sixteen Showings*, the book in which this kindly and devout woman set down the content of her visions.

It is known that she lived from 1342 until about 1430, turbulent years both for the Church, torn by the schism that followed the Pope's return to Rome from Avignon, and for the life of the people who were suffering the consequences of a long drawn-out war between the Kingdoms of England and of France. God, however, even in periods of tribulation, does not cease to inspire figures such as Julian of Norwich, to recall people to peace, love and joy.

As Julian herself recounts, in May 1373, most likely on the 13th of that month, she was suddenly stricken with a very serious illness that in three days seemed to be carrying her to the grave. After the priest, who hastened to her bedside, had shown her the Crucified One not only did Julian rapidly recover her health but she received the 16 revelations that she subsequently wrote down and commented on in her book, *Revelations of Divine Love.*

And it was the Lord himself, 15 years after these extraordinary events, who revealed to her the meaning of those visions.

"*You want to learn the Lord's meaning in all this? Learn it well: Love is the Lord's meaning. Who showed it to you? Love... Why? For Love...* Thus I was taught that Love was our Lord's meaning" (Julian of Norwich, *Revelations of Divine Love,* Chapter 86).

Inspired by divine love, Julian made a radical decision. Like an ancient anchoress, she decided to live in a cell located near the church called after St Julian, in the city of Norwich — in her time an important urban centre not far from London.

She may have taken the name of Julian precisely from that Saint to whom was dedicated the church in whose vicinity she lived for so many years, until her death.

This decision to live as a "recluse", the term in her day, might surprise or even perplex us. But she was not the only one to make such a choice. In those centuries a considerable number of women opted for this form of life, adopting rules specially drawn up, for them, such as the rule compiled by St. Aelred of Rievaulx.

The anchoresses or "recluses", in their cells, devoted themselves to prayer, meditation and study. In this way they developed a highly refined human and religious sensitivity which earned them the veneration of the people. Men and women of every age and condition in need of advice and comfort, would devoutly seek them. It was not, therefore, an individualistic choice; precisely with this closeness to the Lord, Julian developed the ability to be a counsellor to a great many people and to help those who were going through difficulties in this life.

We also know that Julian too received frequent visitors, as is attested by the autobiography of another fervent Christian of her time, Margery Kempe, who went to Norwich in 1413 to receive advice on her spiritual life. This is why, in her lifetime, Julian was called "Dame Julian", as is engraved on the funeral monument that contains her remains. She had become a mother to many.

Men and women who withdraw to live in God's company acquire by making this decision a great sense of compassion for the suffering and weakness of others. As friends of God, they have at their disposal a wisdom that the world — from which they have distanced themselves — does not possess and they amiably share it with those who knock at their door.

I therefore recall with admiration and gratitude the women and men's cloistered monasteries. Today more than ever they are oases of peace and hope, a precious treasure for the whole Church, especially recalling God's primacy and the importance of constant and intense prayer for the journey of faith.

It was precisely in the solitude infused with God that Julian of Norwich wrote her *Revelations of Divine*

Love. Two versions have come down to us, one that is shorter, probably the older, and one that is longer. This book contains a message of optimism based on the certainty of being loved by God and of being protected by his Providence.

In this book we read the following wonderful words: "Clearly God loved us before he made us, and he never lessens that love, and never will. He does all his works and makes all things profitable to us in this love. In this love our life is everlasting. Our beginning is in his love and for his love he made us in him without beginning. We shall endlessly see all this in God. So he taught me to remain steadfast in the Faith and to firmly believe that *all things shall be well.*" (*Revelations of Divine Love*, Chapter 86).

The theme of divine love recurs frequently in the visions of Julian of Norwich who, with a certain daring, did not hesitate to compare them also to motherly love. This is one of the most characteristic messages of her mystical theology.

The tenderness, concern and gentleness of God's kindness to us are so great that they remind us, pilgrims on earth, of a mother's love for her children. In fact the biblical prophets also sometimes used this language that calls to mind the tenderness, intensity and totality of God's love, which is manifested in creation and in the whole history of salvation that is crowned by the Incarnation of the Son.

God, however, always excels all human love, as the Prophet Isaiah says: "Can a woman forget her sucking child, that she should have no compassion on the son of her womb? Even these may forget, yet I will never forget you" (Is 49:15).

Julian of Norwich understood the central message for spiritual life: God is love and it is only if one opens oneself to this love, totally and with total trust, and lets it become one's sole guide in life, that all things are transfigured, true peace and true joy found and one is able to radiate it.

I would like to emphasize another point. The *Catechism of the Catholic Church* cites the words of Julian of Norwich when it explains the viewpoint of the Catholic faith on an argument that never ceases to be a provocation to all believers (*cf.* nn. 304–313, 314).

If God is supremely good and wise, why do evil and the suffering of innocents exist? And the Saints themselves asked this very question. Illumined by faith, they give an answer that opens our hearts to trust and hope: in the mysterious designs of Providence, God can draw a greater good even from evil, as Julian of

Norwich wrote: "So he taught me to remain steadfast in the Faith and to firmly believe that *all things shall be well*" (*The Revelations of Divine Love,* Chapter 32).

Yes, dear brothers and sisters, God's promises are ever greater than our expectations. If we present to God, to his immense love, the purest and deepest desires of our heart, we shall never be disappointed. And *all will be well, all manner of things shall be well.* This is the final message that Julian of Norwich transmits to us and that I am also proposing to you today. Many thanks.

General Audience, 1 December 2010

Pope Francis on the 650th Anniversary of St. Julian's Revelations

I was pleased to be informed that over the course of this year, pilgrims from across the world are gathering in the Catholic and Anglican cathedrals of Norwich to mark the 650th anniversary of the "Shewings" of Mother Julian of Norwich, and I send the assurance of my spiritual closeness to those taking part in the various ecumenical celebrations.

The profound significance of this English mystic for the Christian tradition speaks to us from across the centuries and is increasingly being acknowledged and celebrated. Indeed, her maternal influence, humble anonymity, and profound theological insights stand as timely reminders that faith in God's loving providence and holiness of life expressed in generous service to our brothers and sisters in need, are timeless truths underpinning not only the life of Christian discipleship but the very fabric of a just and fraternal society.

Of particular note is Julian's generosity in welcoming those seeking spiritual counsel and encouragement. This willingness to sacrifice self-convenience for the sake of others is especially needed in responding to the endemic problems of isolation and loneliness felt by so many in the more materially affluent nations of the world. In this regard, it is my hope that through a greater appreciation of the life of Mother Julian, Christians today will be encouraged to follow ever more faithfully and joyfully the example of Jesus, the one who came "not to be served but to serve" (Mt 20:28).

How vital, too, for today's world, is the message of God's mercy and compassion revealed to Mother Julian. In her Revelations of Divine Love, we learn that she was taught through God's grace that, despite the presence of evil in our midst, "*all manner of things shall be well*" (Chapter 32). In this regard, I pray that all who face the pressing challenges of war, injustice, ecological disaster or spiritual poverty, may be consoled and strengthened by these enduring words of wisdom.

To all those participating in the commemorative events, I willingly impart my Blessing, as a pledge of Almighty God's tender mercy and compassionate love for all his children.

Rome, St. John Lateran, 8 May 2023

Chapter I

Introduction to God's Revelations of Love

Sixteen revelations of Jesus Christ's Love, our endless happiness.

It began with his precious crowning with thorns that the Trinity knew and willed at the Incarnate union of a human soul to God, revealing many beautiful insights of endless wisdom and love, the basis of the rest.

In the second his beautiful face changed complexion, an effect of his honorable passion.

The third is on how our Lord—the almighty, all-wise, all-loving God—not only made all that is, but also does and works all things.

The fourth is of copious bleeding at the scourging of his tender flesh.

The fifth is on how Christ's precious passion conquers the Enemy.

The sixth is on how our Lord thanks and rewards his blessed servants in heaven.

The seventh is on the feeling of wellbeing that gladdens us in anticipation of endless joy; and of the woe that warns us of the heavy weight of our fleshly life. Spiritual understanding of God's goodness keeps us secure in his Love, in woe or wellbeing.

The eighth is of Christ's last pains and cruel death.

In the ninth is how Christ's most arduous passion and sorrowful death satisfies the Blessed Trinity, this joyful satisfaction gladdens and consoles us until we come to the fullness in heaven.

In the tenth our Lord Jesus' holy heart is pierced in two, rejoicing in his love.

The eleventh is a profound revelation of his dear Mother.

The twelfth is of our Lord's most worthy Being.

The thirteenth is of how our Lord God's great regard for everything he has done and created, especially man above all his works; the great Satisfaction he made for man's sin, turning our blame into endless glory. In this revelation our Lord says: *Look and see! You will see how the same Might, Wisdom, and Goodness that created all this will restore what is not well.* Finally, God wants us to keep the Faith and truth of Holy Church, so he hides in mystery what we don't need to know in this life.

The fourteenth is how our prayer is founded on our Lord. Our generous response is seen in the two properties: true prayer and steadfast trust. This pleases him as his goodness fulfills it.

The fifteenth shows how all our pain and woe will disappear suddenly, when our Lord Jesus lifts up and rewards us with the joy of heavenly bliss.

The sixteenth is how our maker, the Blessed Trinity, endlessly dwells in our soul in Christ Jesus our Savior to devoutly rule and protect all things mightily saving us from our Enemy, wisely keeping us for love.

Chapter II

Julian's Requests of God

These revelations came to a simple illiterate creature on May 13, 1373. She had asked God for three gifts: first, to know his passion; second, bodily illness in her youth of thirty years old; third, the gift of his three wounds.

While I already had a sense of Christ's passion, God's grace provoked a desire for a bodily experience of our Savior's pains and our Lady's compassion, as did Mary Magdalene and his other true lovers and direct witnesses of his pains. I wanted to be one with them in suffering with him, desiring no other vision or apparition from God until my soul would leave the body. All I wanted was for true knowledge of Christ's passion.

My second request was a contrite and free desire for a severe illness unto death: to receive all Holy Church's rites, that I and all who saw me would think

I was dying, with all its bodily and spiritually pains (with its dreads and tempests of the Enemy) except the expelling of the soul, that earthly life would offer me no comfort. I wanted God's mercy to purge me so as to better live and worship him, to attain a more speedy death, desiring to be with my God soon.

I put one condition on this passion and illness: *Lord, you know I only want your will. If it is not, be not displeased with me.*

My third request was a great desire, by God's grace and Holy Church's teaching, to receive three wounds in my life: true contrition, compassion, and steadfast longing for God. I made this request unconditionally.

So, the two desires came to mind occasionally, but the third was continuous.

Chapter III

The Gift of Suffering with Christ

When I was thirty, God sent me an illness: I laid in bed for days; on the fourth night I received all the rites of Holy Church, thinking I wouldn't last the night. Yet two more days I languished and on the third night I, and those around me, thought I was to die.

It seemed a great pity to die so young and with nothing on earth to live for, yet I trusted God's mercy and feared no pain. I still wanted to live longer so as to know and love God more on earth—this life is so incomparably short compared to heaven's endless bliss. I thought: *Good Lord, does my life no longer honor you?* thinking I would soon die and fully assenting to God's will with all my heart.

This lasted until morning as my body seemed dead, with no feeling from the waist down. With help I tried to sit up, leaning back to enable my heart to more freely do God's will as long as life lasted.

My curate came to be at my last moments; I had my eyes closed and could not speak. He put the Crucifix before my face and said: *I brought you the image of your Maker and Savior: look at him; be comforted.*

I opened my eyes toward heaven, where I trusted to receive God's mercy; as I did I saw the face of the Crucified.

Then my sight began to fail and my room became completely dark as if it were night, I know not how; only the crucifix appeared lit. Beyond it was full of horrors, as if greatly occupied by enemies.

Short of breath and diminishing feelings, my upper body began to fail too. I thought I was truly dying.

Suddenly all my pain stopped and I felt whole as never before.

Marveling at this sudden change, I knew it must be God's doing, not nature's. I felt so at ease, trusting I had gladly been delivered from this world to live no more.

Then I remembered my desire for the our Lord's gracious gift: to experience his blessed passion, for his pains be my pains, with compassionate longing for God, with no desire for any bodily vision or divine apparition, just for my soul to have this natural compassion for our Lord Jesus and to suffer with him.

Chapter IV

Christ's Joy-filled Crown (Revelation 1)

I saw the crown of thorns pressed onto the blessed head of the God-Man, with copious red blood, fresh and warm, trickling down from under the crown, as he suffered his passion for me. This he revealed to me directly.

The Trinity then filled my heart with great joy as though I was in endless heaven. For the Trinity is God: God is the Trinity, our maker and keeper; and our everlasting love, joy, and bliss in our Lord Jesus Christ. In this Jesus appeared to reveal the blessed Trinity.

Benedicite Domine! I said in a reverent and loud voice, amazed and awestruck with reverential fear at his being so at home in the wretched flesh of a sinful creature.

It seemed that God was mercifully preparing me for the enemy's temptations before I died. In the revelation of his blessed passion, my mind saw the Godhead, which was strength enough for me, sufficient for all the living to battle all hell's enemies and temptations.

Our Lord God revealed to me our blessed Lady in her bodily likeness—a humble young maid, in the stature God conceived her, just older than a child, partially revealing the wisdom and truth of her nobel soul in contemplating the greatness of her God and maker, in her littleness as his poor creature. This filled her with reverent fear to marvel at his being born of a lowly creature of his making, moving her to say to Gabriel meekly: *Behold, God's handmaid!* This truly filled her with grace, surpassing everything else God has made; only Christ's blessed humanity is greater.

Chapter V

I Have All in God

Then our Lord gave me a spiritual sense of his most beautiful love, how everything good and enjoyable is found in him, as his tender love clothes us and never leaves us.

From his palm he showed me a tiny, round ball the size of a hazelnut. My mind gazed upon it and asked: What is this? He answered: This is all of creation. I marvel how it remains as it easily could fall into nothingness. He answered: *It remains and shall always endure because I love it, as everything has its being in my love.*

This little thing had three properties: God made it; God loves it; and God keeps it in being. He truly is my maker, my keeper, and my lover; I will never fully rest or be happy until I am united and bonded to him substantially, with absolutely nothing between me and my God.

Compared to our loving and uncreated God, our littleness and nothingness as creatures can make our heart uneasy and restless, seeking consolation in petty things here, while avoiding our almighty, all-wise, all-good God, who is rest itself. For us to know and rest in him pleases God and satisfies us, since no soul rests until it willingly becomes nothing at all for love, so as to have him be our everything. Then it rests spiritually.

God also revealed how a helpless souls, simple and sincere, greatly please him as the Holy Spirit inspires a natural yearning in us: *God, in your goodness you give me yourself: so I want and ask for nothing but you—to worship you fully—for in you alone I have all.*

These words are so dear to the soul, nearly touching God's will and goodness, endlessly comprehending and surpassing all his created and blessed works. For he is eternal and his goodness made us only for himself, his blessed passion restoring us to keep us in his blessed love.

Chapter VI

God's Goodness Is the Highest Source of Prayer

This taught me how our soul must wisely trust God's goodness, asking for help to know and understand Love. It honors and delights God when we faithfully pray and trust his goodness and grace, with true understanding and steadfast love. Prayer is greater than other ways of beseeching, which are too little and fall short of honoring God's goodness fully.

We can beseech by invoking Christ's precious body and blood, his holy passion, wounds, and all the blessed gifts and endless life that flow from his honorable death—all are of God's goodness. We also can invoke his sweet Mother's love in bearing him, which is of his goodness, and the power of the holy Cross on which he died; this too is of his goodness, as is all the honorable help, love, and endless friendship the saints and the blessed company of heaven give us. All these ways flow from the chief one: taking his blessed flesh of the Virgin; yes, everything before and after it pertains to our redemption and endless salvation. So it pleases him that we seek him and worship any way that is of his goodness.

So God's goodness is the highest source of prayer, reaching our tiniest need. It quickens our soul with life, nurturing it in grace and virtue. The soul seeks this grace until he shall enclose it completely in himself. For he loves whatever benefits us and our flesh in the simplest way, for his love made our soul to his own likeness.

As the body is clad in clothes, the flesh in skin, the bones in flesh, and the heart in the whole, so we, body and soul, are clad and enclosed in God's goodness. While all the others waste and wear away, nothing is more intimate, whole, and nearer to us than God's goodness: truly our Lover wants us to fully trust him and his goodness. This pleases God and profits us beyond our heart's imagination.

He so dearly loves and knows our soul beyond all other creatures: in fact, no other creature knows how much, how sweet and tenderly, our Maker loves us. So, with his grace and help, we stand in spiritual awe and endless marvel of God's great and surpassing love for us in his goodness. So we can ask our Lover for anything.

Our nature desires to have God, and God wants to have us, so let's never cease to desire or long for him until our joy is complete and we can desire no more.

For he wants us occupied in knowing and loving until this is fulfilled in heaven. This is the first lesson of love, which gives a strong foundation to all the rest, as we'll see. So by contemplating and loving its Maker, the soul seems less in its own sight, and grows in reverent fear and true meekness that overflows with charity toward his fellow Christians.

Chapter VII

God's Intimate Love Received by Faith

Then I saw a bodily vision of Christ's head with its profuse bleeding: great drops of blood flowed from under his crown like pellets, fresh out of the veins; the blood was brownish-red and thick, becoming bright-red as it spread out; when the blood came to the brow it vanished while the bleeding continued. The drops of blood had incomparable beauty, roundness, and life, flowing profusely like water off the eaves after a heavy rain, countless many drops that spread across the forehead like the scales of herring.

This was moving and life-like, sweet and lovely, yet horrifying and dreadful. Seeing our honorable God and Lord so, simple, and gentle comforted my soul, giving me confidence. He helped me understand with this clear example:

A majestic King greatly honored a poor servant by befriending him, being especially open, sincere, and cheerful with him, both in private and with others. Wouldn't this poor creature think: What more could this noble Lord do to honor and gladden me than to show me such simple and marvelous intimacy as this gives me more joy and pleasure than any gift or external honor?

This revealed how the gentle joy of great intimacy can ravish man's heart such that one can almost forget himself. So our Lord Jesus is with us. Truly this was the greatest joy of my vision, how he—the highest and mightiest, noblest and worthiest: our Father and maker, in our Lord Jesus Christ, our brother and savior—is most intimate and gentle with the lowest and meekest, conferring the marvelous joy in seeing him.

To seek and trust our Lord, to enjoy and delight in his grace will comfort and console us until we see him truly.

Only by a special grace from our Lord and the Holy Spirit can one fully experience this marvelous intimacy in this life. But faith with charity merits and attains this reward by grace; for our life is based on faith, hope, and charity. God gives such a vision to whomever he wills, plainly teaching the same doctrines that we learn from our Faith. So when this vision passes, faith keeps it alive by the grace of the Holy Spirit until our life ends, nothing less or more than as our Lord teaches.

Chapter VIII

Charity for Others

This vision of the profuse bleeding of our Lord's head continued, as did my words: *Benedicite Domine!*

It showed me six things: first, the signs of the blessed passion and shedding of his precious blood; second, his honorable Virgin Mother; third, the Holy Godhead that ever was, is, and shall be almighty, all-wise, all-loving; fourth, how tiny is all that he has made—heaven and earth, all that is great and large, fair and good—to a soul that sees its Creator; fifth, that he made all things for love, keeping them in that love endlessly; sixth, that God is all that is good in each and every thing.

Our Lord revealed this to me in the first vision, with time to behold it. As the bodily vision ceased, spiritual locutions came in my mind, as reverent fear and joy stirred desires to see more, if I dared and if it were his will.

Great charity for my fellow Christian also arose that each might see and experience what I did, especially to comfort those who accompanied me, so I said: *Today is my Judgment Day,* thinking I had died and was to be judged definitively. I also wanted to move them to love God more as life is short, thinking I had received these marvels partly for the sake of my fellow Christians. So I prayed to God for you all, I counseled you to remember this wretch's testimony, and to be comforted in firm, meek beholding God's gentle love and endless goodness, to receive it with great joy and pleasure, as if Jesus had revealed it to each personally.

Chapter IX

"I Am nothing"

I am good not for any vision but for loving God: the more you love the more you are. The wise know this well. I say it for the ease and comfort of the simple, as God didn't reveal himself because he loved me more than other souls in grace—certainly many who only had Church teaching and no vision love God more than I. Alone I am nothing; but I hope to be united in charity with all my fellow Christians.

In this unity, the life of all mankind shall be saved. God showed me how he loves all that is and all that is made as good; so we must love all our fellow Christians as God does. For mankind shall be saved in beholding the maker of all in all that is, as God is in man and in all. May God's grace truly teach and mightily comfort us in beholding him.

To be saved, God reveals that we need to believe only what Holy Church believes, preaches, and teaches.

I have always understood, hoped in, and earnestly maintained—by God's grace—Holy Church's Faith and intend never to receive anything contrary to it. This I diligently hold as one of God's meaning of his visions.

God revealed this in three ways: bodily visions, locutions in the mind, and spiritual insights, which cannot be fully expressed as clearly as I would like. Yet I trust in our Lord God Almighty's goodness to do so more spiritually and sweetly than I could ever.

Chapter X

Christ's Face (Revelation 2)

As I gazed continually on the face of the crucifix placed before me with a bodily vision of Christ's passion, his face would change colors despite the spitting, buffeting, and many languishing pains, more than I could ever tell. First I saw half the face, from the ear to the mid-face covered with dry blood. Then I saw the other side similarly covered, while the first side vanished.

I saw this bodily, troublesome and dark. I wanted it to last, to see it more clearly. He responded in my head: *To see more, let God be your light: nothing else is needed.* So I sought him.

It is so blind and foolish not to seek God until his goodness shows himself to us. When we do see him, grace moves us to great desires for even more.

I saw him and sought to have him more. This should be our common task in this life. Continual seeking pleases God greatly, as the travail of seeking is as good as finding: the Holy Spirit uses the faith and hope our seeking, travail, and trust to confer charity and clarity—the special grace of finding when God's wills it. This glorifies God as the Holy Spirit's grace and light confers the profit meekness and virtues on a soul. Only by the trust of seeking and finding fastens a soul to God, glorifying him, according to my vision.

Then I was led in mind to the sea's bottom where I saw green hills and valleys, with moss, seaweed, and pebbles. I understood that if one were under the deep sea yet could see God, his body and soul would be unharmed and safe, since God is continually with him, having more solace and comfort than this world could ever give. To see him continually, God wants us to believe, though it seems little: it will confer even more grace: to see him, seek him, abide in him, and trust him.

This second vision was so short and simple that it disturbed me greatly, making me sad, fearful, and longing; I even doubted for some time whether it was a vision. Then I understood that our blessed and beautiful Lord—no one was ever so beautiful as when travail, passion, and dying changed the color of his face—truly gave this vision as a figure and likeness of how he bore our sins and foul deeds. I thought of Veronica's Holy Veil in Rome and how it portrays his blessed face changing color as he steadfastly endured his passion and death: sometimes it became more attractive and life-like, sometimes less so and death-like. I marveled at how a sorrowful and emaciated image could portray the blessed Face's heavenly beauty: an earthly flower, fruit of the Virgin's womb. God's grace would reveal it to me in the eighth revelation.

By faith we know and believe Holy Church's teaching and preaching, that the blessed Trinity made man to his image and likeness. Yet when man fell wretchedly into deep sin, we also know that nothing but his maker could restore him. As God made man for love like unto the Trinity, only his love could restore man to the surpassing bliss of love, remaking us like Jesus Christ, our Savior, in heaven without end.

Thus he took to himself our mortality and wretched foulness out of love and for our glory to remove our guilt. This is what he meant when I sensed that *our blessed and beautiful Lord truly gave this vision as a figure and likeness of how he bore our sins and foul deeds.*

In every seeking soul in grace accompanied with discretion and the Holy Church's teaching I saw three things common: first, earnest and diligent seeking, without sloth, unreasonable hesitance or vain sorrow; second, steadfast abiding in his love to the end, without murmuring or complaining as life last but a while; third, complete trust and faith in him, knowing that he shall appear suddenly and blissfully to all who love him.

For he works in secret, wanting to be perceived and trusted, as his appearance will be swift and sudden. For he is all gracious and beautiful: O Bless him!

Chapter XI

Doing All Things Well (Revelation 3)

Then I saw God in a point while in all things, giving me a soft dread to think: *What is sin?*

God is involved in everything, even the tiniest, as nothing happens by chance but his wisdom foresees it all: a thing may seem to us to be by chance due to our limited foresight, it is not so for God's limitless wisdom, which foresees all things justly and continually, leading them to their best end.

Everything that happens must be good, as our Lord God does all, working in creatures as the center-point of all things. Sin is the working of creatures. So, I am certain he sins not.

I saw how sin is truly nothing. Yet I marvelled not at this, but at how God's justice works in souls.

Justice has two beautiful properties: it is right and just, as are all our Lord God's works, needing no mercy or grace: for nothing of his fails.

In another vision I saw sin simply, and how God's mercy and grace works.

All our Lord's works are completely good, gentle, and sweet, leading us from blind foolishness to his sweet wisdom. For man sees some deeds as good and others as evil, but our Lord sees only what has created being and is of his doing. It is easy to see what is a good deed as our Lord ordained both the highest or lowest and properly ordered each from the beginning; there is no doer but he.

I am absolutely sure that his purpose will always remain unchanged in everything, as his justice preordains all from the beginning, setting each in its order as it was to remain without end; this includes every single kind of thing, for he made all things good and all his works are pleasing to the blessed Trinity.

So happy was he in revealing this he said: *See, I am God! I am in all things and do all things! I never lift my hands from my works, and never will, as I lead all things to the end to which I ordained them, by the same power, wisdom, and love whereby I made them! How can any thing be amiss?*

In lovingly contemplating this, my soul felt compelled of great reverence to assent God's joy.

Chapter XII

Christ's Bleeding Body (Revelation 4)

Then I saw Christ's body bleeding profusely from the scourging with deep wounds in his tender flesh and sharp cuts covering his sweet body. Hot blood flowed so profusely one could hardly see any skin or wounds, but only blood. When the blood was about to fall, it vanished. The bleeding continued for a while that I might contemplate it; it was so profuse that it should have flooded my bed completely.

Then God's tender love for us came to mind, how he made plentiful waters to cover the earth for our service and bodily drink. Now he wishes to give us his blessed blood to drink and wash us of sin. Most bountiful and precious is his dear love in the outpouring of his blood is for us and our nature.

His precious blood is so bountiful that it even descends into hell to burst the bonds of all who belong to the heavenly Courts! It overflows the Earth, to wash away the sin of all men of goodwill—past, present, and future. His honorable blood also ascends to heaven to the blessed body of our Lord Jesus Christ to bleed before the Father to beseech him for us until we enjoy the salvation of the appointed number of mankind.

Chapter XIII

Conquering Satan (Revelation 5)

Before revealing any words, God allowed my soul time to take in the meaning of what I had seen. Then, without voice, my soul intuited these words: *This*—the blessed passion—*conquers the Enemy,* revealing that the passion overcomes the Enemy, who still exudes the same malice as before the Incarnation but is now frustrated seeing souls saved and escaping by the virtue of Christ's precious passion. This fills him with shame and evil, which God allows for our joy. And this happens as much when God lets him acts as when he doesn't let him, because he never harms us as he would like: for God holds all the power.

God has no wrath. As I saw it, our good Lord helps all those he saves to profit in his endless glory. His might and right withstands the Reproved as he fights against God's will in his malice and wicked deeds. Our Lord wants us to scorn his powerless malice, so I laughed mightily, as did those who accompanied me, which gave me joy. I wished that all Christians would laugh with me. But Christ didn't laugh. Yet we can, as a way to comfort ourselves and rejoice in God who conquers the devil, which he scorns. This led to an inward insight of truth, without his changing appearance, how God is always the same.

I then became serious and said: *I see three things, game, scorn, and earnest*: *game*, as the Enemy is conquered; *scorn*, is how God treats him; *earnest*, our Lord Jesus Christ's earnest travail of his holy passion and Death to conquer him.

God scorns and condemns the Enemy now and without end, as at Judgment day. God frustrates him, seeing all the saved and by how all the woe, pain, and tribulation he attempts to inflict on us falls back upon himself to increase our endless joy as he burns in endless hell.

Chapter XIV

Our Reward (Revelation 6)

Our good Lord said: *I thank you for your travail, especially in your youth.* He raised my mind to heaven where I saw our Lord, master in his own house, calling all his dear servants and friends to a great feast. The Lord took no seat in his own house yet royally reigns in it with a lovely and happy face, filling his true and noble friends with endless celebration, gladness, and intimate comfort with marvelous songs of endless love. The Godhead's glorious face fills the heavens with joy and bliss.

God confers three degrees of heavenly joy on every soul that willingly serves him on earth in any way. First, his great honor and thanks delivers the soul from pain; such honor so fills the soul that it desires nothing more. For all the pain and travail that all men suffer wouldn't deserve such honor and thanks that just one man receives for serving God willingly. Second, how all in heaven sees the honor and thanks for each soul's service, as his example shows the king greatly honoring and thanking his servants in front of all in his realm greatly increasing the honor. Third, a new endless happiness.

This insight was so beautiful and sweet, how every man's age and time of serving will be known and rewarded in heaven, even more those who willingly and freely offer their youth to God.

For when a loving soul truly serves God and his eternal will, God gives him these three decrees of joy, even more as the soul serves him gladly throughout his life.

Chapter XV

Reassuring Peace (Revelation 7)

Then God gave my soul a great spiritual joy: everlasting assurance free of any dread. I felt so happy, at peace and rest, that nothing on earth could grieve me.

This lasted but a while, then life's great weariness returned. I was so weary I hardly had strength to live, with only my faith, hope, and charity to comfort me in truth, but with no feeling.

Again our blessed Lord gave me holy comfort, rest, and a strong assurance free of bodily dread, sorrow, or pain. Yet again I felt pain, then the pleasing joy… back and forth, about twenty times. In joy I could say with Paul: *Nothing can separate me from Christ's love*; and in pain, with Peter: *Lord, save me, I'm perishing!*

My mind saw how comfort sometimes benefits a soul and other times by being left alone. God wants us to learn that he keeps us secure in both woe and health, and how being left alone is not always due to sin, but can benefit a soul without sin. Yet I don't deserved the bliss I experienced—our Lord's one love he freely gives when he wills.

God reassures us of his everlasting and surpassing bliss, when he will wipe out all pain for those who are saved. God doesn't want us to focus on our pain or mourn our sorrow, but for us to overcome them quickly to possess endless enjoyment.

Chapter XVI

Christ's Dying (Revelation 8)

Christ then showed the part of his passion as he approached his death.

I saw his sweet face bloodless and dry in pale dying, languishing the more as he turned deathly blue; and then brownish-blue, as his flesh approached death. I saw this chiefly in his lips, which had been fresh, ruddy, and pleasing, now they took the pitiful colors of death, with their moisture clotted and dried, seeing his fair, life-like color turned black and brown.

As his sweet body bled out all his precious blood, his body dried up from within that he might die, yet some moisture remained in his sweet flesh. Cold wind blew from without which also hastened the drying of his flesh that seemed to dry part after part, with incredible bitter and sharp pains. As long as Christ's flesh had any life he suffered.

His dying lasted to the point of suffering the last pain: his sweet body became so discolored, dry, shrunken, and pitiful as if he had been continually dying for seven nights. The thought of Christ's drying flesh was the most painful and enduring of his passion.

Chapter XVII
"I Thirst"

Seeing Christ's dying, his words, *I thirst,* came to mind. His thirst was double: bodily and spiritual.

His bodily thirst was due to a lack of fluids, leaving his blessed flesh and bones without blood or moisture as his body dried. The twisting nails in his tender sweet hands and feet bore the weight of the body, as the grievous nails enlarged the wounds of the sagging body's lengthy hanging. Also the piercing and pressing of the crown binding his head, caked with blood clinging to his sweet hair, dry flesh, and the thorns that tore the flesh and enlarged the wounds. I saw his sweet skin, tender flesh, and blood soaked hair hanging loosely over the bone like sagging cloth that would soon fall off into many pieces. The thought of this possibility filled me with great sorrow and dread, but the sharp thorns of the crown were so tightly set in the pierced bone that it didn't happen. After awhile this began to change; I marveled to see him begin to dry so as to carry the weight at the crown of dry clotted blood enveloping the crown of thorns. The skin of his face and body were slightly rippled with a tanned color, like dry, aging wood; the face was browner than the body.

His body dried in four ways: first in loss of blood; second in the subsequent pain; third, exposure to the air, like clothes hung to dry; fourth, his unquenched thirst in all his woe and distress. His pain intensified as the moisture failed and he began to dry and shrivel.

He showed me the pains of his blessed head: his body's slow drying up by the blowing wind from without, with unimaginable pain and cold. His pains are so indescribable it is better left untold.

This vision filled me with only a feeling of Christ's pain, which seemed to surpass bodily death. I know well he suffered but once, but he showed it to me to fulfill my earlier desire, knowing so little of what pain meant; for had I known I would never have prayed for it.

I thought: What pain is like this? I heard in my heart: *Hell is worse, a pain of despair. But the greatest of all salvific pain is to see your Love suffer, who is your life, your bliss, and your joy.* What pain could hurt more? I truly felt I that I now loved Christ more than myself that I could suffer no pain greater than to see him in pain.

Chapter XVIII
All Creation Suffers with Him

Then I saw our Lady's compassion, so united to Christ in love that it brought her great pain. All creatures naturally love him but his sweet Mother, augmented by grace and her higher and sweeter love, much more so, producing pains surpassing all others', seeing her beloved in such pain.

All true lovers and disciples suffer this pain more than their own bodily dying, as my experience confirmed, the least of those who love him.

Here saw I a great union of Christ with us: when he is in pain, we are too.

All creatures that suffer do so with him: in fact, as God has made all earthly and heavenly creatures to serve us, their nature succumbs to the pain and sorrow of Christ's dying in response to their God: when he fails their virtue fails in mutual solidarity, to the extent they can.

So all his friends—and all creatures except the mighty from whom God hides it—also suffer with him for love: those who don't know him suffer various discomforts. Some are like Dionysius the Areopagite, a pagan awestruck witnessing Christ's horrific suffering, saying: *Either the world has come to an end or our creator suffers.* Returning to Athens he inscribed on an altar: *Altar to the Unknown God.* God's goodness—which makes the planets and elements, the blessed and the cursed—had withdrawn from both, such that those who knew him not suffered too.

So for us our Lord Jesus became nothing, and all of us with him until we enter bliss with him.

Chapter XIX

"Jesus, You Are My Heaven"

My eyes remained fixed on the Cross; for I was safe and secure from our frightful enemies, as long as I looked at the Cross, and didn't want to put my soul in peril by turning away from it.

Then my mind heard as from a friend: *Look up to heaven to his Father,* and, with eyes of faith, I saw that nothing between the Cross and heaven could harm me. Feeling the need to respond, I answered inwardly with all my might: *But you are my heaven,* preferring to remain in that pain until Judgment day than to look up and go to heaven without him, so tightly I felt bound to him. Thus by his grace, I chose Jesus in his passion and sorrow to be my heaven. I wanted no other heaven than him in his pain; he will be my bliss.

This has always comforted me in health and woe.

Wretched creature I am, as I had said how had I known how painful this would be, I would not have prayed for it. Yet God did not blame my flesh for its frail reluctance without assent. I felt compelled to choose between two contraries: one, to flee flesh's outward pain, woe, and death in this life—which I felt and repented of a lot at this time—or to seek the elevated holy life of peace and love, a more inward, mighty, wise, and steadfast life by choosing Jesus as my heaven.

I saw the inward way as true master over the outward, freeing my intent and will to be united to our Lord Jesus. The outward way repulses the inward, but by grace the inward draws the outward to unite them both in endless bliss in Christ's virtue.

Chapter XX

Pain Becomes Endless Joy

Our Lord's languish was lengthy, as his divine love strengthened his humanity to suffer more than any man could, in fact, more than all men together who would be saved, from the first to the last day, more than the most painful and horrific death of the most honorable king. For he, the highest and worthiest, became nothing and most utterly despised.

What makes the passion so great is the one who suffers it, his great nobility and glorious divinity, united to his most tender and blessed body, so lofty, tender, and pure to suffer such severe pain.

He suffered for everyone's sin, experiencing each one's sorrow and desolation due to blindness and love. (Even our Lady suffered his pains, and more he, being greater and worthier in nature, hers). Even now risen and impassible, he suffers with us.

His grace strengthened my love for him, seeing how Christ willingly chose to endure his passion that surpassed all pain with great desire and pleasure, turning all pains into everlasting joys.

Chapter XXI
Contrite Compassion

God wants us, strengthened by his grace, to view the horrific sufferings of his blessed passion with contrite compassion.

I awaited his departing and the vision's end thinking he had died, but he hadn't. As I looked at the same Cross, his blessed countenance changed, as did mine, becoming joyful and happy, as my mind heard our Lord say merrily: *Where now is your pain or grief?* I was full of joy.

With his help and grace, we are called to willingly abide in our Lord's pains, passion, and dying, to where he suddenly gives us his joy to be with him in heaven. Between one moment and the other no time shall transpire. So he said: *Where now is your pain or grief?* We shall be fully blessed.

His holy joy reveals how no earthly pain, sorrow, or travail should bother us, as it all leads to the joy and bliss of sharing his life, passion, and cross, as our frailty allows, so that his goodness could raise us up with him in bliss; as our little suffering now will lead to a more exalted, endless knowing in God beyond what we'd have without it. So the greater our pains with him on the cross, the greater our glory in his Kingdom.

Chapter XXII

Love Made Him Suffer More (Revelation 9)

Jesus Christ then asked: *Are you glad I suffered for you?* I said: *Yes, good Lord, thank you! Blessed are you, oh Lord!* Then our kind Lord said: *If you are glad, I am too: it gives me endless joy, bliss, and satisfaction to suffer the passion for you; and if I could've I would've suffered more.*

This lifted my mind to marvel greatly at the three heavens in Christ's blessed humanity, yet none was more or less, or higher or lower, but all equal in bliss.

In the first heaven, Christ revealed his Father's character and action reflect in Christ, without bodily likeness. The Father rewards his Son Jesus Christ with gifts so holy… nothing pleases the Father more than what Jesus does for our salvation. This pleasing the Father is complete heavenly bliss. Yes we are his because he bought us, but also because the Father kindly gives us to him as his reward, honor, and crown. (What a singular and delectable marvel to be his crown!) All his cruel and shameful travail, passion, and death seem nothing but a great bliss to Jesus.

While Christ's sweet humanity could suffer but once, his goodness never ceases: as he is ready to do it again for love. He told me that to make a new heaven and new earth is little compared to what our Lord God did for man's soul: to die for his love. Then he said: *Should I not die so often, despite its hard pains, as I did it for your love? It is worth it all!*

The words, *if I could've I would've suffered more*, showed me how he often came close to dying but his love didn't let him—the number surpassed my wit and reason, yet it all was so little to do for love.

In his blessed passion, his love made him suffer beyond all his pains, as far heaven is above the earth. It was all nobly and honorably driven by love, a love without beginning or end. As he said so sweetly: *if I could've I would've suffered more*. He didn't say, *had I needed to suffer more…* for even if it were not needed, he would've.

God perfectly ordained the work of our salvation confer full bliss in Christ: bliss wouldn't be full, if it could be better.

Chapter XXIII

A Glad Giver

The words: *it gives me endless joy, bliss, and satisfaction*, revealed three heavens: the Father is pleased in *joy*, the Son is honored in *bliss*, and the Holy Spirit is *satisfied*.

Our kind Lord revealed his holy passion to me in five ways: in his head's bleeding; in his facial discoloring; in his copious bleeding from the scourging; in his extended dying—these four are the pains of the passion; fifth, in the joy and bliss his passion brought.

God wants to comfort and strengthen our soul so as to be merrily occupied with him, enjoying our salvation with him in his grace. For his joy is to be endless with us and we with him.

Nothing God does, has done, or will ever do for us costs him, except what he did in our humanity, from his Incarnation and to his blessed rising on Easter-morn: he did it all to redeem us who he endlessly enjoys.

Jesus wants us to appreciate the blessed Trinity enjoying our salvation, and for us to enjoy it spiritually as much as Christ does.

The whole Trinity embraced Christ's passion, showering on us abundant virtues and grace, yet only the Virgin's Son suffered to the endless joy of the whole blessed Trinity, as he said: *Are you glad I suffered for you?* In other words: *If you are glad, I am too… it gives me endless joy, bliss, and satisfaction to suffer the passion for you; and to make you happy*.

Then I thought: a glad giver values what he gives little, seeking only to please and solace the one who receives the gift with great gratitude; a kind giver simply forgets the costs and efforts at the joy and delight of the one he loves. This was fully revealed to me.

The word *forever* reveals the greatness of his love in saving us (from endless pains of hell) by his passion, how what he did produces such manifold joys over, yet he will suffer no more.

Chapter XXIV

A Glance at His Wounded Side (Revelation 10)

Then our Lord glanced at his side and rejoiced. This led my mind to his pierced wound, revealing a beautiful and pleasant place big enough for all the saved to rest in peace and love. It also came to mind his blessed pierced heart, pouring out his precious blood and water for love, revealing the blessed Godhead's endless Love, with no beginning or end. Joyfully our good Lord said: *See how I love you*, as if to say: *My dear, see how your salvation gives your Lord, God, and Maker endless joy, bliss, and satisfaction, for my love rejoice in it.*

These blessed words helped me understand: *See how I love you! I love you so much that I would do it again willingly: all the bitter pain, travail, and death for you. It has now all become endless joy and bliss. Ask for anything that pleases me, would I not gladly grant it to you? Your holiness, joy, and endless bliss with me, all please me.*

The blessed words, *See how I love you,* meant all this to me. Our good Lord simply desires to make us happy.

Chapter XXV

Our Lady (Revelation 11)

With celebratory joy our good Lord looked down to his right, to where our Lady stood during his passion, asking: *Would you like to see her?* as if to say: *I know you would, for after me my blessed Mother is the highest joy I could show you, my greatest pleasure and honor, and the most desired sight to my blessed creatures.* I marveled at his great and singular love for this most blessed Virgin Mother, Holy Mary, her great joy at those sweet words, as if to say: *Do you see how I love her, that you might enjoy my love for her and hers for me?*

To help us understand these sweet words, our Lord speaks to all the saved as to one person: *See how I love you in her! For I made her great, noble, and so worthy of your love; this pleases me as it should you.*

For after himself she is the most pleasing sight.

I longed to see her bodily, but saw only her soul's virtues: her truth, wisdom, and charity so as to know myself and reverently fear my God. So when our good Lord had said those words: *Would you like to see her?* I responded: *Yes, good Lord, thank you, if it is your will.* When I said this, I thought I would see her bodily, but did not. Instead Jesus revealed a spiritual vision of her to me: while before I had seen her lowly and simple, now I saw her exalted, noble, and glorious, pleasing to him above all creatures.

He tells us that pleasing her pleases him. To help me understand he gave me an example of a man who wants all creatures to love and please the great love he loves above all others. This is why Jesus asked: *Would you like to see her?* This thought and spiritual insight was the most pleasing he could have given me. On three occasions our Lord revealed to me our Lady, Holy Mary: when she was with Child; in her sorrows beneath the Cross; and now in her pleasing, honor, and joy.

Chapter XXVI

It Is I (Revelation 12)

Then our Lord revealed how our soul shall never rests until it rests in him, who is the fullness of joy, beauty, kindness, holiness, and life itself.

Our Lord Jesus often said: *It is I, it is I: it is I in the highest; it is I whom you love, whom you enjoy, whom I you serve; it is I for whom you long and desire, who means everything to you; it is I who is all. It is I whom Holy Church preaches and teaches, it is I who reveals himself to you here.* How such words entered my mind and senses to comprehend, I cannot say, but they brought insurpassable joy to the heart or soul. So while words are insufficient, may God give everyone the grace to receive what our Lord intends by them.

Chapter XXVII

Why God Allows Sin (Revelation 13)

The Lord reminded me of my earlier longing to never sin. I had thought: had sin not entered the world all of us would still be clean just as our Lord made us.

So, I often wondered, in folly, why God's great foreseeing wisdom hadn't prevented sin from ever beginning, as then everything would've turned out well. I tried to let go of this thought, but sadly I couldn't.

But Jesus revealed what I needed to know: *Sin was bound to happen, but all shall be well, yes, all shall be well, and all manner of things shall be well.*

While *sin* includes all forms of evil and shameful deeds, it is utterly nothing. Yet he bore this nothingness for us in his spiritual and bodily pains and death, and in the sufferings of all creatures (for we follow Jesus, our Master, until we are fully purged of the nothingness of our deadly flesh and lack of goodness in our inward affections). I saw all the pains that ever were or will be, including those of Christ and his passion, in an instant that quickly passed to comfort: for our good Lord would not let my soul fear this terrible vision.

As sin has no element of substance or being, it is only known by the pain it causes. While pain lasts a short time, according to my revelation, it purges us, helps us know ourselves, and moves us to seek mercy. In all this our Lord's passion comforts all to be saved with his tender love; while sin causes all pain, *all will be well.*

In no way did these tender words blame me or any of the saved. So it is unreasonable to blame God, wondering why he allowed sin.

Why he did remains a great marvel and mystery that only God knows. He will manifest it to us in heaven, in our endless joy of seeing him.

Chapter XXVIII

Our Lord's Compassion for Us

As the sight of Christ's passion had filled me with pain and sorrow, now I saw Christ's compassion for us due to sin, filling me with compassion for my fellow Christians and for all to be saved. This will shake God's servants, Holy Church in sorrow, anguish, and worldly tribulation, like men shaking a cloth in the wind.

Then our Lord said: *This shall be something great for endless honor and joy in heaven.*

I saw our Lord's delight and compassionate remorse in his servants' tribulations, while the world blames, despises, mocks, and rejects each person he loves, he lays no blame but mitigates the injury of this wretched life's pomp and vainglory, making the way easy to everlasting bliss in heaven. As he says: *I shall obliderate your vain desires and vicious pride, uniting you to me: meek and mild, clean and holy.*

All charitable compassion one has for his fellow Christian it is as for Christ.

Both in his passion as in his compassion, he wills for us joy and happiness, and comforts us in our pain—we never suffer alone but always with him. His pains and nothingness are beyond anything we could ever suffer, turning our pain into honor and profit.

This will help us not to murmur or despair in our pain, as his merciful love and kindness pardons what our sin truly deserves and dispels all blame, looking with pity as upon innocent and industrious children.

Chapter XXIX

Christ's Satisfaction Surpasses All Sin

I pondered and mourned our troubled world. Fearfully I dared to ask for clarity: *Good Lord, how can all be well when sin causes such great harm to creatures?*

Our blessed Lord responded delightfully, showing how Adam's sin harmed the world more than any other since until the end of time, as the Church universal clearly teaches, and how his glorious satisfaction and reparation pleases and glorifies God more than any harm from Adam's sin. So, our blessed Lord concluded: *If I make well the most harmful then much more will I make well all that is less so.*

Chapter XXX
God's Privy Truth

God's truth has two sides: one regards our Savior and our salvation: it is open, clear, beautiful, and comprehendible to everyone of good will, binding us to God as the Holy Spirit draws, counsels, and teaches us inwardly, just as Holy Church does outwardly in the same grace. The more we joyfully strive to fully embrace his truth with meek reverence the more we delight our Lord and the more his grace fills us to readily enjoy our part in him. The other part of this truth goes beyond our salvation and remains hidden from us, privy to our Lord and God in his royal peace counsel. His servants ought to obey and respect him without having to know his counsel completely, yet it pleases him, and unburden us more, to trust him and not busy ourselves in these things. The saints in heaven only want to know our Lord's choosings, ruled by our Lord's will alone; so should we too, seeking our Lord's will alone: we are all one in God's sight.

This taught me to trust and rejoice in our Savior, blessed Jesus, in all things.

Chapter XXXI

Lasting Spiritual Thirst

Our good Lord answered all my concerns about his statement: *I may make all things well, I can make all things well, I will make all things well, I shall make all things well; and you will see how all manner of things shall be well.*

When he said, *I may*, he meant the Father; and *I can*, the Son; and *I will*, the Holy Spirit; and *I shall*, he meant the unity of the blessed Trinity, three Persons and one Truth; and when he said, *You shall see yourself*, he meant the union of all those saved by the blessed Trinity. God wants these words to put us at rest and peace.

Christ's spiritual thirst and love-longing shall end with the beatific vision on Judgment day, as the saved (some who have died, some here, and some to come) enjoy Christ's bliss. Then his thirst and love-longing will unite us all together in his own bliss, according to my vision. For we are not yet in him as fully as we shall be.

Our Faith teaches, and God reveals, that Christ Jesus is both God and man. As God he is, was, and shall ever be in highest and endless bliss that never increases or decreases. I saw this clearly in every revelation, and especially in the twelfth where he says: *it is I in the highest.* Our Faith and God's revelation says that, as man, he suffered and died in a love that is also divine, to bring us to his bliss. God rejoices in the work of Christ's humanity, as he said in the ninth revelation: *it is a joy, a bliss, an endless satisfaction for me to suffer the passion for you*, as *we are his bliss, his reward, honor, and crown,* the bliss of Christ's works.

Christ our Head is glorified and impassible, but we, members of his Body, are not yet fully glorified or impassible. Yet the longing and thirst that he had on the Cross remain until the last soul to be saved reaches salvific bliss.

Mercy and longing are both proper to God, as Christ longs for us, so we too must long for him: no soul goes to heaven without it. Such longing and thirst comes from God's endless goodness, just as compassion and pity do. Christ's spiritual thirst and pity, shall cease as our need for them ends on Judgment day. All this was seen in the revelation on his compassion.

So his longing for us, with its suffering love and compassionate mercy, does not end until the time is ripe.

Chapter XXXII

God's Great Salvific Act

Our good Lord had said: *All shall be well,* and *you'll see for yourself all kind of things shall be well.* These words can have several meanings.

First, that he values little, lowly, and simple things as he does great and noble ones; the tiniest thing shall not be forgotten and *shall be well.*

Second, as evil deeds cause such great harm—that some would never reach the beatific vision of the Blessed Trinity and God's high marvelous wisdom, power, and goodness—making it seem impossible to ever be made well; all this filled me with sad remorse, since our reason is so blind, lowly, and simple. Yet he said: *you shall see for yourself all kind of things shall be well,* as if to say: *Just be faithful and trust, then you shall see it in the fullness of joy.*

These words: *I shall make all things well…*, and his works yet to come, comfort me as our Lord revealed how on the last Day the blessed Trinity shall do a great Act, now hidden from all creatures until it happens. God's goodness, love, might, and wisdom wants this Act to remain concealed from us to put our soul at ease hin his peace and love so that such troublesome things wouldn't keep us from truly enjoying him and trusting that he *shall make all things well.* For just as the Blessed Trinity made all things out of nothing, it shall make well all that is not well.

Our marvelous Faith is founded on God's word and teaches that everything in God's word shall be fulfilled. The Faith teaches that many creatures shall be condemned: the angels that fell from heaven due to pride, becoming God's enemies men too who died without Holy Church's Faith or who abandoned Christian life to die without charity: all these shall be condemned to endless hell. So it seemed impossible for *all kind of things shall be well*, as our Lord revealed.

Our Lord God responded simply: *What is impossible for you is possible for me: My word shall save all things and make all things well.* So he taught me to remain steadfast in the Faith and to firmly believe that *all things shall be well.*

In this Great Act our Lord's word shall save and make well all that is not well. No creature knows or shall know how until it is done; this is what I understood of our Lord's meaning.

Chapter XXXIII
Admiring All God's Acts

I dared to ask to see hell and purgatory, not because I needed proof of anything pertaining to the Faith, for I do indeed believe that hell and purgatory exist, as Holy Church teaches, but to learn and live my Faith better and to worship God more fruitfully.

All my desires seemed now as nothing. The first vision had shown how God reproved and endlessly condemned the devil and all his followers. After that only the devil is mentioned.

God reveals his goodness, hardly mentioning evil: the revelations of Christ's passion—the first, second, fifth, and eighth, where I partially sensed our Lady's and his friends' sorrow seeing him in pain—showed nothing of those who put him to death. Still in Faith I knew that, without the grace of conversion, they would be forever accursed and condemned. This encouraged me to remain faithful in all I had understood, hoping in God's merciful grace to keep me until life's end.

God wants us to respect all his deeds, especially his Great Act. Let us imitate our fellow saints in heaven, seeking only God's will, happy in what he hides and in what he reveals, not occupied in knowing his secrets, which only distances us from knowing them.

Chapter XXXIV

God Hides Things for Our Sake

Our Lord revealed two kinds of mysteries. One—this Great Act—God will hide until the time he chooses to show us. Other mysteries our blind ignorance hides from us; but his mercy reveals them in the Holy Church's preaching and teaching, to help us know, love, and trust him more, making them easy for us to learn.

Meekly embracing Holy Church's preaching and teaching pleases God, who is its foundation, its substance, its teaching, its teacher, its end, its reward for the soul's every travail.

Every soul to which the Holy Spirit declares shall know these. I truly hope all will profit by them as they seek God.

The third revelation comforted me against sin: seeing no sin as God does all: so *all is well* and *all shall be well*; more on this later.

Chapter XXXV

Trusting in God's Justice

As God's plentiful Goodness so joyfully reveals these things, I sought assurance that a certain soul, whom I loved, would continue in the good life he had begun by God's grace. This desire for a special revelation seemed to hinder me. Then I heard in my mind, as from a friend: *Look at the Lord God's graciousness towards you. It honors God more for you to see him in all things than in some particular thing.* Thus I learned how it honors God more to trust him in all things than to take pleasure in knowing every detail. Not knowing special details should cause neither gladness nor distress: for *All shall be well.* True joy is to see God in all: for by the same blessed might, wisdom, and love he made everything, and our good Lord continually leads it all to the same end. I saw this in the first revelation, and more clearly in the third where I saw God in a point.

What our Lord does is good and true; we must respect all that he allows, whether good or evil. This doesn't mean that evil is honorable but that our Lord God's goodness and marvelous meekness suffers it to reveal his endless mercy and grace.

God is just, and all his justice and works are unsurpassably right and good, as his great might, wisdom, and goodness pre-ordain them in a continual act with one end that fully pleases him in everything. This fills the soul of the saved with sweet and blissful grace that leads it to heaven with its endless vision of God, to the marvel of all creatures.

So mercy is God's goodness constantly at work in just souls who experience sin's hostilities. Mercy will cease when sin's hostilities do while justice remains forever. He allows us to fall, but we are saved in his holy love, might, and wisdom as his mercy and grace raise us to more manifest joys, making his justice and mercy known and loved, now and forever. So the soul that wisely beholds his justice in grace will pleasantly enjoy both with endless joy.

Chapter XXXVI

All God's Acts Are Good

Our Lord God said that he acts even if I did nothing but sin, as sin doesn't hinder his goodness. It brings even more heavenly joy to God-fearing souls who desire his will. His action will begin here and glorify God, bearing much fruit in his earthly lovers; in heaven we'll marvel in joy until the last Day, while the glory and bliss endure in heaven before God and all his holy ones forever.

Our Lord mentions his great Act for us to rejoice in him and in all his works. It will be something great and blissful, which we should accept with faith and trust, even while he keeps it secret from us.

Certainly he doesn't want us to fear what he reveals, but for it to help us love and enjoy him more. All he does is glorious and fruitful for us in his love. His goodness keeps somethings privy, for us to trust and enjoy in his endless bliss. So let's rejoice in what he shows and what he hides; if we do so meekly we shall have great peace in endless thanks.

When he says what shall be done *for me,* he means, *for all to be saved.* What God does shall truly glorious and marvelous, of the highest joy. Man only contributes sin to God's Act, as he says: *Look! See the way to meekness, love, and nothingness so as to enjoy me in my love: this pleases me most.*

Often in this life we foolishly look at the reproved, yet our Lord tenderly calls us: *Give me all your love, my dear child: turn to me—I am enough for you—enjoy your Savior and your salvation.* Thus our Lord works in us. Not only understanding souls will see and feel God's grace working in them, but all men without exception. What it will be remains hidden from me.

But this Act is really two: one is known to whom our Lord grants at their going to heaven. Yet the Great Act on earth can only be known when it is done.

He also gave me special teaching on miracles, saying: *I have done many and diverse miracles, high and marvelous, glorious and great. As I have done, I do continually, and will in the time to come.*

There is sorrow, anguish, and tribulation, to manifest our weakness and woundedness due to sin, to make us meek, God-fearing, and to seek his help and grace. God's great might, wisdom, and goodness, produce miracles for us to experience a sliver of heaven's virtue and joys in this passing life, strengthening our faith and hope in charity. He is known and glorified in miracles for us to bear harsh sorrows and trials.

Chapter XXXVII
Sin Turned to Glory

Seeing our Lord and his merciful grace in me was so pleasant, yet God reminded me that I would sin. As I took this personally, he graciously comforted me, referring to all Christians in general would sin, not just me.

A gentle dread hit me, but then our Lord responded with indescribable love, security, and assurance: *I'll keep you safe*, comforting me for all my fellow Christians, as God loves all to be saved as one soul. This makes me love my fellow Christians more.

The soul to be saved has a godly will in the higher part that doesn't assent to sin and can will only good, no evil; the lower part has a beastly will that can will no good.

Our Lord shows that we stand in his full love; his endless love for us pleases him: yes, he loves us both here and now, and when we'll be before his blessed face. True travail is to fail to love.

Chapter XXXVIII

Examples of Sin Turning to Glory

Man's sin leads to glory, not shame. While he punishes sins with various just pains as to their gravity, God gives the same soul a level of heavenly joy and bliss to the level of pain and sorrow it experiences on earth. As each soul is precious and honorable to God his goodness would never allow a sinner's soul to go to heaven without rewarding sin's pain with endless bliss and surpassing glory.

He then lifted my mind to heaven where he showed me David, and countless saints of the Old and New Law: Mary Magdalene, Peter and Paul, Thomas and Jude of India, and countless others: all sinners yet without shame. Thus our kind Lord showed how our sin is turned to glory.

For intimate comfort our Lord reminded me of St. John of Beverley, a dear neighbor I knew who became a great saint in heaven. In his honorable youth he served, loved and feared God greatly, yet God allowed him to fall while mercifully keeping him from perishing. God then led him to meek contrition, surpassing the grace he would have had had he not fallen. All this was confirmed with many miracles done by his body.

Our Lord revealed all this was to make us happy.

Chapter XXXIX

God's Mercy for Sin's Scourge

For a chosen soul, sin is the severest scourge, making it repulsive even to itself and deserving of hell. When the Holy Spirit moves it to contrition, its wounds heal and its bitterness turns into hope of God's mercy and the soul revives in the life of Holy Church. The Holy Spirit leads us to confess our sins simply and truly, with great sorrow and shame for defiling God's fair image. Through our confessor, Holy Church enjoins on us a penance for every sin, as the Holy Spirit teaches. Its meekness moves God's mercy greatly, as does its bodily sickness, sorrow, shame, reproof, humiliation, anxiety, and temptations.

When our sin makes us feel deserving to be forsaken and discarded, our Lord takes us as his treasure, raising us in our meekness high in his sight by the grace of great contrition, compassion, and true longing for

God, delivering us quickly from sin and pain to take us up into bliss, making us even as great saints.

Contrition cleanses us; compassion readies us; true longing for God elevates us. By these means all sinners shall be saved and go to heaven, healing the soul. Once healed, God sees the soul's wounds as badges of honor: while sorrow and penance punish us, God's almighty love rewards us in heaven for our travail—no one will lose out. For God looks upon sinners with a lovers' sorrow and pain, with blameless love alone. The reward shall be great, glorious, and honorable, as shame turns into joy and glory.

Our kind Lord doesn't want us to despair over frequent or grave falls, which don't hinder him from loving us. Peace and love are always present and at work in us, even if we don't feel them. He wants us to make him our life's foundation, everlasting keeper, and powerful defender against our enemies of love; we need him more the more we fall.

Chapter XL

Divine Friendship

Our kind Lord tenderly keeps a royal friendship with us while we are in sin, gently urging us to expose our sin to his sweet mercy and grace. But seeing our foulness and anticipating God's punishment for our sin moves us to contrition, prayer, and desires to amend our life mightily so as to appease God's wrath, put our soul at rest, and calm our conscience. Then hope in God's forgiveness fills and gladdens the soul as our kind Lord welcomes us as friends just released from prison, saying sweetly: *My darling I am glad you come to me: I have been with you in all your woe and now we are united in bliss and love.* Thus mercy and grace forgives sins as our soul experiences joy—a foretaste of heaven—fruit of the Holy Spirit's gracious work and Christ's passion.

God's great goodness prepares our need for true peace, charity, and salvation. As we will always lack such fullness in this life, we strive to increase our prayer, longing, and thirst for our Lord Jesus, just as he longs and thirsts to bring us to the fullness of joy.

No one should falsely think: *It is good to sin so as to increase one's reward and lesson one's guilt.* No! True love hates sin. The more a soul experiences our Lord's kind love the more it abhors and loathes sin. For the pains of sin are worse than those of hell, purgatory, death, and any earthly suffering. Sin is utterly vile, despised beyond anything that is not sin. Sin is hell; the harshest hell possible.

We rely on love, meekness, mercy, and grace to make us fair and clean. God's mighty wisdom willingly saves us. All Christian laws teach us to do good and avoid evil, and are founded on Christ, who is charity itself, as he acted as we should act, for he wants us to be like him in full and endless love: only his love can break us of our sin and self-love so as to love our fellow Christian. So let us hate sin and endlessly love souls as God does. Then his words, *I keep you secure,* become endless comfort.

Chapter XLI
Prayer and Thanksgiving (Revelation 14)

Our Lord then gave me two conditions for prayer: justice and complete trust.

Trust is lacking when we doubt that God hears us due to feeling unworthy nothingness or barren dryness in our prayers. But my experience is that such feelings are folly and the cause of weakness.

Suddenly our Lord said these words in my mind: *I am the foundation of your prayer: first I will that you pray; I move you to will to pray; finally you pray. So why would anyone not pray?*

This comforted me greatly: saying, *you pray*, shows how prayer pleases him greatly and will be rewarded. Asking, *why would anyone not pray?* shows how not praying for mercy and grace is foolish, for our good Lord ordains and moves us to entreat him for everything. Clearly our prayer doesn't cause God's goodness;

instead his sweet words, *I am the foundation…* lets his lovers on earth know this so as to pray all the more; this is what our Lord meant.

Prayer is the sweet inward work of the Holy Spirit uniting and binding the soul's true and gracious will to our Lord's. Gratefully our Lord takes our prayer, as I saw it, to enjoy it in the heavenly treasury where it never perishes but is continually received before God and all his saints, to meet our needs, increasing our joy and bliss in endless glory and thanksgiving.

Prayer pleases our Lord whose grace makes us like himself through it, as he says: *Pray, even if you don't get anything out of it, or even if you feel that you can't pray, for it is profitable. For if dry or barren, or in sickness or weakness, or you get little out of it, prayer is very pleasing.* He desires and rewards with endless thanks our believing and continuous prayer. God accepts his servant's goodwill and travail, despite how we feel. It pleases him that we work at our prayers and at being good by grace and reasonable discretion, directing our powers to possess Jesus, whom we seek, in the fullness of joy. As he revealed in the next revelation: *I shall be your reward.*

Prayer includes thanking: an inward, reverent recognition that moves us to do what our good Lord wants with great inward energy. We can exclaim: *Thank you, good Lord, bless you!* Or when our heart feels dry and empty, or tempted by the enemy, reason and grace moves us to recall our Lord's blessed passion and great goodness, as his powerful words and grace quicken our heart to act rightly, pray joyfully, and enjoy our Lord, leading to blissful thanks in seeing him.

Chapter XLII
Trusting Prayer

Our Lord reminds us of prayer's three elements: first, prayer arises from him, as he said: *I am the foundation…* and: *It is my will.* Second, prayer identifies our will with his, as he said: *I move you to will to pray.* Third, prayer's fruit and end is union with our Lord in his likeness in all things. *May he be ever blessed for* this lovely lesson*!*

Our Lord wants our prayer to be both trusting and generous, for without trust—if we delay our prayer or find it tedious—we don't truly honor our Lord because it fails to acknowledge our Lord's grace and love as the foundation of our prayer. So, after God first gives us mercy and grace to ask, we must trust to obtain all the gifts we desire in his true mercy and grace.

But let's not be down if we pray a lot but don't get what we asked. Surely our Lord has a better gift, time, and more grace in store for us. He wants us to fully know him and his Being, as to enlighten our mind with the gracious light of creating us; second, of redeeming us; third, of making all things to serve and preserve us. It is as if to say: *And I have done all this before you ever prayed. Now pray.* His greatest deed he has already done, as Holy Church teaches, and we should give thanks and pray for all that he continues to do to rule and guide us to his honor in this life and in the bliss to come. So, he does all.

He does all this for us to pray. Once is not enough. If we become sad and doubtful that will do it, we dishonor him. If we trust that he will do it without praying, we sense no debt to him.

Let's thank and honor him as soon as we see our prayer fulfilled. Our Lord ordains everything for us to pray, to share his unimaginable joy and bliss in thanksgiving and honor.

Prayer helps us understand and have sure hope in the fullness of joy to come and to which he kindly ordains. Until then our understanding love longs for and trusts in our Savior. His goodness, which continually beholds us, draws us to long for and trust in him.

So be diligent—which is so little—in asking for mercy and grace to find all we need in him. In saying: *I am the foundation of your prayer*, he conquers all weakness and doubtful fear.

Chapter XLIII

Prayer Unites Us to God

While sin distances us from God's likeness, grace restores the soul, in nature and substance. Prayer draws the soul to will as God wills and comforts its conscience, opening it to grace. So, he teaches us to pray with firm trust that we shall obtain it. His Love wants to partner with us in doing good, moving us to pray for what he wants to do. Our prayer and good will are his gift for which he will give us endless reward.

This is why our Lord said: *Finally you pray,* revealing his great pleasure, as though he were indebted to us for all the good deeds we do (really he it is who does it) by firmly praying to do what pleases him. Thus he says: *Nothing pleases me more than for you to pray wisely and earnestly for me to do what I shall do.*

So prayer unites us to God.

But when our kind Lord graciously shows himself to our soul, we have all we desire. When we don't see him, we pray more, with attention and effort wholly on seeing him. This prayer is hardly perceivable, as I saw it, as it focuses on seeing him to whom we pray, on marveling and enjoying him with reverent fear and sweet delight, praying for nothing but to have him who moves us; the more the soul sees God the more it desires him by his grace.

Yet if we don't see him we must pray, for we lack what fills our very self: Jesus. If we are overwhelmed, troubled, or feel unrest we must pray, docile and obedient to God. (But our prayer doesn't change God, who is always in love).

If we pray for certain needs our good Lord comes to help. Yet by a special grace he may show himself clearly without us praying for anything. Then we follow him, drawn to his love as his marvelous and plentiful goodness fills all our powers to do all kinds of good, wise, and unimaginably great things such that all we do is to behold and enjoy his goodness, delighting in his love with desires to be fully united to him in his presence.

His sweet grace, inspirations, and spiritual affections meekly spur us on to pray to him continually in this life, much more than our simple heart can bear. The Holy Spirit does this until we die in longing love and come to our Lord, where we know ourselves and him clearly, fully possessing God and all things in him: to see, hear, and experience him in a delightful inbreathing and sweet tasting of him.

Then shall we see God face-to-face, intimate and full, to behold him endlessly, whom no man can see in this life and live. But he may show himself here by a special grace to strengthen us as hs wills.

Added Insights to the First 14 Revelations

Chapter XLIV

Sovereign Truth, Wisdom, and Love

In these revelations, God shows how man can exercise his will to worship without sparing anything, as marvelously seen in how Truth and Wisdom worked in Holy Mary's soul (see ch. 4). May the Holy Spirit now show us how.

Truth sees God, Wisdom beholds him, and from these arises Love, a marvelous holy delight in God. God's endless, sovereign, and uncreated Truth, Wisdom, and Love creates man in his image with these same properties, so as to see, behold, and love God, so that God and creature enjoy each other in endless marvel.

Man marvels in seeing his great God, Lord, and Maker incomparably high and good. The creature scarcely seems worthy of himself, yet Truth and Wisdom enables him to see and reflect that he is made for endless Love, which God preserves in him.

Chapter XLV

Two Ways of Judging

God justly and endlessly sees and safely preserves our natural being one and whole in him, whereas we, in our changing body, judge outward appearances that move from one thing to another. This obscures man's judgment: sometimes it is good and easy, and sometimes hard and painful. Our good Lord Jesus reforms us, letting the mercy and grace of his blessed passion work to bring us to justice.

He unites both judgments into one, as it'll be forever in heaven. The first is of God's justice in living in our humanity; then the sweet judgment of his beautiful Revelation. God blamelessly assigns both to us, which is sweet and delightful. While Holy Church will occasionally judge sinners of blame and wrath, these are not in God. The higher and lower judgments, as taught by Holy Church, can't be laid aside. So I longed to reconcile how both judgments can be correct and honorable in God, and how Holy Church's judgment is true.

Our Lord answered me in a marvelous example of a lord and his servant—as we will consider shortly. Yet I still desired to know how these two judgments applied to me and how all things heavenly and earthly are grasped in them. The Holy Spirit leads us to get to know our failings so as to long, by nature and grace, for perfection in endless joy and bliss. God created our natural being from the beginning to be endlessly holy in God.

Chapter XLVI
Knowing Our True Self

In our passing life, our sense-soul doesn't know our true self well. The more we do the more we will see and know our Lord God in the fullness of joy and the more we shall long for our bliss, both by nature and by grace. We come to know our true self in this life by exercising and growing our higher natural powers, as we respond to God's mercy and grace, but we know our true self fully only at the anguish of death. So we should long, both by nature and grace with all our might, to know our true self fully in endless joy.

Our Lord's grace helped increase my higher knowing and loving in two ways: first, in all his revelations to me he showed me his endless and constant love, assured of perseverance and salvation; second, in their consistency with Holy Church's teaching in which my mind and will were formed, keeping me steadfast in every way, called to love them and find them good.

Despite this I felt drawn to learn how we deserve pain and wrath for our sins and for the good deeds and obligations we fail to do. Yet our Lord showed no anger, and never will, for God is good, life, truth, love, and peace with no room for anger or anything else contrary to his might, wisdom, and goodness; he is only goodness. Our soul is united to unchangeable goodness—to the God of all goodness—arousing neither wrath nor forgiveness; absolutely nothing separates God from our soul.

In every revelation, love led my soul to the truth of his great goodness. God wants us to learn as much of this as simple creatures can. For God reveals what he wants us to know and keeps secret what we shouldn't know until the time we are ready. So happily I embraced our Lord's marvelous will and yield to my Mother, Holy Church, as a simple child ought.

Chapter XLVII
True Mercy

Our soul has two duties: to reverently marvel and meekly suffer while enjoying God, as will become clear.

I pondered: *What is God's mercy and forgiveness?* I understood God's mercy as forgiveness of sin producing wrath. For a soul desiring only love, nothing hurts it more than God's wrath. So forgiveness of his wrath made sense as mercy's main focus. Yet nothing God revealed indicated this, as God's grace showed how his mercy works on frail, weak, and foolish man who is changeable and has to struggle against sin in this life. This is beyond man's blind will to do alone: unable to see God causes difficulty, sorrow, and woe. For being able to see God would eradicate temptations and desires to sin.

This vision was higher, fuller, and more gracious than anything I had ever felt in this life; yet it still seemed small and low compared to my great desire to see God.

I felt five things: *joy, mourning, desire, fear,* and *sure hope. Joy* in seeing God; *mourning* for my failings; *desire* to see him forever in heaven, as we never fully rest until we do in him; *fear* that my vision might soon end and I'd be left alone; *sure hope* in his endless love and mercy, preserving me for his bliss. My *joy* comforted me in the *sure hope* of his mercy, alleviating all *mourning* and *fear*. Sensing that this vision might soon end, as visions of God do in this life when we turn in on ourselves with the rebelliousness of the ancient first sin and subsequent connivances that produce travail, anguish, and other spiritual and bodily ills in this life.

Chapter XLVIII

God Has No Anger

Our good Lord, the Holy Spirit—God's endless life dwelling in our soul—keeps us secure in his peace, bringing us the ease of grace, uniting us to God in obedience. Our Lord's mercy continually works during this changing life.

Wrath—bold opposition to peace and love, arising from weakness, ignorance, or evil— I only saw in man, whom God forgives, not in God himself. Instead his lovely respect, compassion, and pity show how his mercy works by preserving us in love.

I only saw this aspect of God's mercy in my visions.

Mercy is a sweet gracious work of love and pity that preserves us, turning all things into good. God always keeps his sweet eye of pity and love on us even as we fail, fall, and even die, yet to work his mercy conquers our dreadful and shameful sorrow.

Mercy and grace are simply two forms of love. Mercy pertains to tender, motherly love: nurturing and preserving life, healing and suffering too. Grace arises from the same love: endlessly raising and rewarding beyond what our longing and travail deserves, revealing the great generosity of God's royal lordship and marvelous kindness. This abundance of love turns our failing, falling, and dying into full and endless solace that rises into a holy and honorable life.

As hostile wrath brings earthly pain, shame, and sorrow, grace brings us solace, honor, and surpassing bliss in heaven as its sweet reward for which we'll thank and bless our Lord, endlessly rejoicing in every suffering endured. We can't fully know God's blessed love without experiencing the suffering first.

In all this, it became clear that God's mercy and forgiveness lessens and destroys our anger.

Chapter XLIX

God Vanquishes Anger

I marveled at how clear it was that anger is impossible in God. We are endlessly united to him in love; our life is founded and rooted in love, for without it we cannot live. As wrath opposes friendship and love, he destroys our wrath to unite us to himself in his gentle love and meekness.

As our Lord clearly is the peace that vanquishes all wrath. Were God angry even for a moment our life would cease and our being, vanish. For God's endless might, wisdom, and goodness gives life and preserves us in being. While failures make us feel wretched, God's mild meekness enclose us in his kind goodness, reassuring us of endless friendship, life, and being in him.

If we sin, God's endless goodness keeps us from perishing, offering us peace to calm our perverse wrath at falling. This helps us see our need for true fear, forgiveness, and desires for salvation. While rebellious wrath and blind frailty cause painful trials, God's mercy secures us, safely preserving us in being. Yet we are only safe and happy in endless joy when God's goodness completes our peace and love, pleasing him in all his works and judgments, loving what God loves, at peace with ourselves and our fellow Christian.

Thus God is our peace and sure keeper. His mercy and grace bring us back to endless peace when we are restless, making us meek, mild, secure, and at peace, uniting our soul immediately to God who has no anger. Our Lord's goodness bears fruit of peace and love as it vanquishes all our rebellious wrath that only produces trials and tribulations; these our Lord Jesus takes to heaven with him to make them unimaginably sweet and delectable, filling us with endless glory in heaven where we'll be as he is: unchangeable. God is the firm foundation of total bliss.

Chapter L
Blameless in God's Sight

Mercy and forgiveness is the way that leads us to grace in this life. Falls, trials, and sorrows make us seem dead to earthly eyes, yet to God we are never, ever dead.

This made my whole soul wonder and marvel, thinking: *Good Lord, I know you are Truth itself and how daily we sin gravely: How is it that we have no blame? I know Holy Church's teaching and feel the guilt of sin, from the first man until we reach heaven.* Our Lord God surprised me, reaffirming how we have no more blame than do the clean and holy angels in heaven. So these two contraries bothered me greatly due to my blindness, fearing that I may lose his blessed presence while still not knowing how to look at sin. For it seems that God totally destroys sin with nothing to link our guilt. I longed for the revelation to endure, yet I lacked the patience for such perplexity, thinking: *If I affirm that we are not guilty sinners I would err and fail to acknowledge the truth. Good Lord, how can I not see this truth in you, my God and maker, in whom I desire to see all truth?*

Three reasons drove my inquiry: first, because it is so basic, were it not I would be afraid; second, it is so common, for were it special and secret I would also be afraid; third, to live here, I thought, I need reason and grace to love the good and hate evil, as Holy Church teaches. With all my might I cried inwardly for God's help, saying: *Oh Lord Jesus, King of bliss, how shall I be at peace? Who shall teach me what I need to know, unless I see it in you?*

Chapter LI

A Lord and His Servant

Our kind Lord then revealed the full mystery by a wonderful example of a lord who had a servant, giving me spiritual and bodily understanding without bodily likeness.

God showed me a lord who sat at a stately rest and peace; a servant reverently stood before his lord, ready to do his will. The lord looked on his servant with love and sweetness, as he meekly sent him out to do his will, which the servant does with great eagerness and love he falls into a deep ravine and is gravely injured; he groans, moans, and struggles, unable to get up or help himself in any way.

What hurt the most was not being able to turn his face to see his loving lord, who was so close to him yet he could only focus on himself and on his human sufferings.

He suffered seven great pains: his bruising from the fall; two, his body's heaviness; three, the feebleness from the first two; four, a blind and stunted reason, barely remembering love; five, inability to rise; six—the most amazing to me—his loneliness with nobody to help; seven, the location where he laid on was long, hard and steep.

I marveled how this servant had meekly suffered all this. I diligently searched for any fault or blame in him but found only goodwill and eagerness that provoked the fall, just as he was when he stood before his lord ready to serve. The lord continually looked upon his servant with tender love. God gave me two perspectives: an outward vision of great compassion and pity, and an inward and spiritual one where I saw God's great joy and glory in restoring his servant to full grace in a second vision.

But our kind Lord told me in the first vision: *Look, my beloved servant has endured such harm and distress with goodwill service in my love. Should I not reward him for all his painful suffering, and not give him more glory than had he remained unhurt? Or do you think I should not grace him at all.*

He then gave my soul a spiritual insight of how his great goodness had to reward his honorable and beloved servant in glory beyond what he would have had he not fallen, turning his fall and woe into greater and surpassing glory and endless bliss.

While the vision vanished, my marvel over this example never left me. As it answered my questions, I still lacked the ease of full understanding, as this marvelous example took time to fully sink in. The servant was certainly Adam but with three things remaining in marvelous mystery: the initial teaching; second, the spiritual insight that helped me understand it; third, how all the revelation of this book were so inseparably united that they had to be held and trusted as one, for our Lord God, in his goodness, reveals and declares them to us for the same end it is his will.

New Insights 20 Years Later

Twenty years later, I had a spiritual insight concerning these things. While they remained a mystery, I freely and firmly assented to all that I saw at that time: the lord and his servant, how and where the lord sat, the clothes they wore, their outward figure and countenance, and inner nobleness and goodness, and the servant's industriousness.

I understood that the lord, sitting stately at rest and peace was God and the servant, Adam. After his fall the servant was all of us, for in the vision of all men are as one, and one man as all: injured, feeble, dazed, and unable to see his lord. While God willed that he'd be whole, man remained hindered and blind, filled with great sorrow and distress to not see his loving lord and thus from seeing his true self as loved by his meek and mild lord, who would bring him true peace leading to the fullness of heavenly bliss in his grace.

Thus I came to know how he views our sin: while pain blames and punishes, our kind Lord's compassion comforts us in his joyful love as he draws us to his bliss.

The lord sat in a simple place on bare ground, alone in the wilderness; his clothing was ample and dignified, as proper to a lord, and its color was a deep, somber blue; his spirit was merciful; his face was tan and his eyes were black and beautiful—both his were attractive, full of lovely compassion, respect, and heavenly bearing. His loving gaze upon his servant was constant, especially in his fall, melting our hearts for love and joy, infinitely surpassing anything on earth. The Father had a marvelous combination of heavenly compassion, pity, joy, and bliss—compassionate pity for his most beloved creature, Adam in his fall, and joyful bliss for his glorious Son, who is with the Father. The merciful sight of his loving countenance filled the earth, even down to Adam in hell, where Adam was kept from endless death by God's ongoing mercy and pity for us until we go to heaven.

The Lord and his Servant

We are blind in this life, unable to see God our Father as he is. When his goodness wills to show himself to us, he does so intimately as man, yet we know and believe that the Father is not a man.

Sitting on the barren ground in the desert shows how he made our soul, his most pleasing work, to be his city and dwelling-place. So when we fell into sorrow and pain, it seemed that God the Father could prepare no other place for himself, sitting upon the ground waiting for mankind, now mingled with earth, until his glorious Son's hard travail would bring noble beauty back to his City. The lord's blue clothing reflects steadfastness; his beautiful tan face and black eyes reflect holy soberness; his full, beautiful, and flaming garments reflect all the heavenly joys and bliss enclosed within him. The Father sat at rest and peace as lord with authority over mankind, as the Godhead toils not.

Seeing this I said: *Our Lord allowed me to see his great rejoicing and glory in restoring his servant to the fullness of his grace.*

I marveled at the lord's stately bearing with his servant standing reverently before him. The servant was clad as a simple laborer ready for work, standing very close to the lord, slightly to his left. He wore a single, white tunic—strait-fitting and short (a hand-width below the knee); it was old, threadbare, stained from sweat, seemingly ready to be torn to rags. I marveled at how the servant was unseemly clothed yet so greatly loved to stand before so honorable a lord. The servant's love for his lord was equal to the lord's love for him.

The wise servant anticipated his lord's needs and how to honor him, then did it all eagerly for love, disregarding himself and what could befall him. His clothing showed he had been a laborer for long time, yet the servant was young.

The lord had a treasure that he loved. Wondering what it was, I heard the answer: the earth and its delectable food, pleasing to the lord who the sat as a man without meat or drink to satisfy him. I was amazed at how this majestic lord had only one servant, whom he sent, wondering what kind of work could one servant do. I came to understand that he was a gardener, doing the hardest work with toil: to dig, till, and plow the earth and water the plants. So the servant travailed, sweating profusely to bring noble and ripe fruits before the Lord, and serve him and his desires, not resting until the food to please his lord was prepared; all the while the lord sat in the same place, waiting for his servant.

The Servant is Three

The lord had all goodness and endless life, longing only for the servant to prepare the earth, his treasure, and present it to him to be glorified in the Lord's deep and endless love. So beyond the lord there was only wilderness. I still didn't get what this example all meant, wondering who the servant was.

The servant is three: the Second Person of the Trinity, Adam, and all man. The Son is equal to the Father in his Godhead; the servant standing on the left of the lord refers to Christ's humanity from Adam. The lord is God the Father; the servant is the Son, Christ Jesus; the Holy Spirit is their mutual love.

When Adam fell, God's Son fell, due to his intimate union with man. The Son's humanity is inseparable from Adam and from all man. Adam fell from life to death, into the ravine of this world and then into hell: God's Son fell into the ravine of the Virgin's womb, Adam's fairest daughter, to excuse Adam of blame, both in heaven and on earth, and to mightily deliver him from hell.

God revealed both his own Son and Adam as one man. The servant's wisdom and goodness pertains to God's Son; the servant's poor cladding belongs to Adam and to our humanity's feebleness. Any virtue and goodness in the servant is due to Jesus Christ; any feebleness and blindness, to Adam.

Our good Lord Jesus took on all our blame; the Father cannot blame us any more than he would his own glorious Son who, before coming to earth, was the servant standing ready before the Father—yet he is equal to the Father in the Godhead—intending to come at the proper time to bring mankind back to heaven. Foreseeing that he would become man to save man by doing his Father's will, he stood before his Father as a servant, resolutely taking on all our debt. To fulfill the Father's will, he fell into the Virgin's womb, disregarding himself and his sufferings.

His single white tunic is the flesh, as nothing separates it from his divinity; short, strait-fitting, worn, old, and sweat stained shows Adam's poverty and the travail of the servant's labor.

I heard the Son saying: *Lo, dear Father, I stand here in Adam's tunic ready to run to earth to glorify you. When will you send? How long must I wait?* As God, the Son fully knows when the Father wills it and how long he must wait, for he is the Father's Wisdom; so this question regarded his humanity, as his sweet Incarnation and holy passion will save all mankind, for he is the Head and we, his members. The day and time when every woe and sorrow shall end as we reach everlasting joy and bliss is unknown to his members; all heaven's company longs to see that day, and everyone under heaven shall come forth, with longing desires, as reflected in the servant's standing before his lord—i.e., to the Son's standing before the Father in Adam's tunic. Jesus longed to save us all: Jesus IS all to be saved, and with God's charity, and man's obedience, meekness, patience, and virtues, all to be saved IS Jesus.

I learned this marvelous example as if it were my A B C's, with mystery remaining in all the revelations. The servant's standing reflects our travail; being on the left, our unworthiness to be before the lord; he runs from the Father to the Virgin's womb, and fell by taking on our flesh, experiencing our deadly pains. In uncomely laborer's garb stood before the lord as inferior, not resting until he won his peace rightfully with hard work. The Father willed his own Son's humanity, not sparing him from our pains in the blows, scourging, thorns, nails, and the renting of his tender flesh (as I saw earlier how his flesh was rent from the skull until the bleeding ceased and it began to dry and cleave to the bone)—all reflected in the servant's ragged and rent tunic, in his struggle, writhing, groaning, and moaning. After falling into the Virgin's womb, he could not rise until he had died, yielding the soul into the Father's hands with all mankind for whom he was sent.

He powerfully descended into hell to raise up our great ancestors and unite them to himself in heaven. His body laid in the grave until Easter-morn, now to live forever, ending his struggle, pain, groaning, and moaning. God's Son took to himself our deathly flesh—Adam's old, short, threadbare, strait-fitting tunic—to heal and beautify it, making it new, white, and clean; wide and long, marvelously fair and rich like the Father's blue honorable clothing.

The Son sits not on an earthly desert but on the most noble and pleasing throne in heaven. He no longer is a poorly clad servant naked before a dreaded master, but stands before the Father in blissful garments and with a rich crown. For we, in our marvelous, eternal bliss in heaven, are his crown that enriches the Father's joy, the Son's glory, and the Holy Spirit's pleasure. The Son stands not as a laborer on the Father's left, but sits at his Father's right hand in endless rest and peace (not side by side as we do in this life—as there is no such sitting in the Trinity—but at his Father's right hand, in the noble heights of the Father's joys). God's Son, true God and true Man, is the Spouse at peace with his beloved and beautiful virgin Wife of endless joy, sitting in rest and peace in the City his Father built according to his eternal design. The Father is in the Son, and the Holy Spirit is in the Father and the Son.

Chapter LII

One Life in Jesus and Adam

I saw God rejoicing as our Father, Mother, and true Spouse of our soul, his beloved Wife. I saw Jesus Christ rejoicing as our Brother and Savior. God wills us five great joys: to enjoy, praise, thank, love, and endlessly bless him.

In this life, all to be saved have a marvelous blend of health and woe, of the glorious risen Jesus and the wretched wound of Adam's fall and dying. The touch of Christ's grace makes us steadfast, assuring us of salvation in the broken darkness of Adam's fall and our various sins and pains. Let's abide in God, faithfully trusting in the mercy and grace he works in us. His goodness opens our mind to see: in Adam we fall; in Christ we rise.

In us such feelings are so thoroughly blended that we hardly know ourselves and where we stand, or our fellow Christians. But in the same holy assent we make as we sense God drawing our heart, soul, and will to him, we also come to hate and despise all evil promptings and occasions of sin. While we see and feel love working by grace, we hate nothing but sin—love and hate are the two great opposites. Our Lord led me to understand that we can't completely avoid sin in this life, as we will in heaven. Holy Church teaches that grace can keep us from sin and endless pains, but we can only avoid venial sins to a point, as our wretched blindness weakens us and we fall—as sweetness is hid our blindness returns, as do various woes and tribulations. Yet we can readily rise as grace heals our will, especially of grievous sin, to go quickly to God in love without discouragement, despair, or reckless indifference to sin. But faith comforts us, knowing that Christ's virtue resists and avoids us assenting to evil promptings, prayerfully enduring pain and woe until he returns. Admitting our feebleness allows us to live only by grace, reverently trusting in God alone.

This tension remains, yet we trust that he stays with us throughout our life in three ways: drawing us to himself as true man in heaven (seen in vision on Spiritual Thirst); leading us on earth (as in the revelation of God in a point); endlessly dwelling in, ruling, and preserving our soul (seen later in the 16th revelation).

While the servant was scathing and blind from Adam's fall, I also saw the wisdom and goodness of God's Son and the lord's compassionate pity for Adam's woe, and how the honorable Son's passion and death would bring great nobility and endless glory to mankind. It pleased him to raise man from his fall and confer on him full bliss, surpassing what man would've had without the fall. I saw this simultaneously with the fall.

Now we have reason both to morn and for enduring joy: our sin caused Christ's pains yet his endless love led him to suffer.

I beheld God first, then man; our Lord asks us to meekly accuse ourselves for God's goodness to excuse us. Seeing how the lord beheld his beloved servant's fall in a very meek and mild manner, with compassionate pity and endless love, we come to discover God's everlasting love and generous mercy if we meekly accuse ourselves of our falls and of the irreparable harm they do. Thus the Lord's works in our lower part after man's sorrowful fall and our Lord's reparation.

The inward way is higher and more complete, as natural love and grace confer virtues of our higher part over the lower. Nothing can divide one from the other, for love is one yet works doubly in us: his great love and joy in the higher part benefit our lower part in relieving its pains and passions with mercy and forgiveness, by turning our guilt and blame into noble and endless glory.

Chapter LIII

Christ's Humanity Unites All

To God, the fall of any creature to be saved is no greater or lesser than Adam's, who was endlessly loved and kept secure in his need, as we know, and is now blissfully restored in surpassing joy. For our good Lord is so gentle and kind that he will never fault those he shall ever bless and praise.

So the lovely lord and servant vision partially answered and eased my great dilemma. I learned that every soul to be saved comes to have a godly will that would never assent to sin or evil, but only to good in God's sight. Our Lord teaches this to keep our will whole and safe in faith in our Lord Jesus Christ. For when our human nature is fully in heaven it'll be so bonded to his substance to make it inseparable from him, fulfilling his own good will and endless purpose.

While we need to be redeemed of our sin, this endless bonding is just, as Holy Church teaches the Faith.

For God always loved man, desiring our endless bliss, fulfilling God's joy in all his works. God's sight has always been on man, known and loved from the beginning in his endless assent. The whole Trinity is in full accord with the Second Person being foundation and head of our fair nature: we all are enclosed in him, come out of him, and go with him to heaven's full and eternal joy, as the blessed Trinity always foresaw. For before he made us he loved us; then we love him. The Holy Spirit's substantial goodness is to be the Love of the Father's might and of the Son's wisdom. Thus man's soul is made by God and is bound to God.

While God made man's body out of the clay of earth—the matter of all bodily things—God made man's soul out of absolutely nothing that is made. This is how all created nature is united to its Maker—uncreated substantial Nature. So nothing separates God from man's soul.

God teaches, and all his revelations show, that man is his noblest creation, that Christ's human soul is of the fullest substance and highest virtue, preciously knit to him by a subtle but mighty knot and endless union at creation, and finally that all souls to be saved in heaven are knit to this union and are made holy in his holiness.

God keeps man's soul whole in his endless Love, which draws us to him, never to be lost. Our soul is alive by his goodness and grace drawn to endure in heaven: to endlessly love, thank, and praise him who treasured and hid us in God, knowing and loving us from without beginning or end.

Chapter LIV

Love Unites Us to God

God's love for man is great and endless, as God's love for Christ's blessed soul is inseparable from his love for the least soul to be saved. It is easy to believe that Christ's blessed soul fully dwells in the glorious Godhead, so where Christ's soul is, there is the substance of all the souls that he saves.

The truly wise inwardly see and know that God dwells in our soul—let us rejoice that God made our soul to be his dwelling! But there is still greater wisdom and joy to know that our soul dwells in God, and that he made our soul for it to dwell in the substance of the uncreated God; we are of and for God's divine substance.

So, I saw no difference between God and our substance: yet God is God and our substance is his creature. For the Trinity's almighty truth is our Father who makes and keeps us in him; the Trinity's deep wisdom is our Mother, enclosing us all; the Trinity's goodness is our Lord, dwelling in us and we in him. We are enclosed in the Father, in the Son, and in the Holy Spirit, and each is enclosed in us: he is our one, almighty, all-wise, all-good God and Lord.

The Holy Spirit infuses in the sensitive part of our natural being the virtue of faith (and with it all virtues): for true belief, right reason, and sure trust is that we are in God and God in us. God ordains this and the others virtues working great mercies in us, graciously uniting us to Christ through the Holy Spirit's gifts and virtues so as to live as Christians, Christ's children.

Chapter LV

Christ Is Our Way

Christ is our secure Way, his laws leading us mightily to heaven in his body. To save us, Christ devoutly appears with us before his Father in heaven, who receives us thankfully, kindly giving us to his Son, Jesus Christ as a gift. Thus we become the Father's joy and the Son's bliss that pleases the Holy Spirit. It pleases our Lord greatly for us to share the blessed Trinity's joy (as revelation 9 shows). Whether we feel ill or well, God teaches us to believe that we are truly more in heaven than on earth.

Faith begins in our soul's natural love, enlightening reason with a steadfast mind; this God confers when he first makes us, breathing a soul into our bodies as mercy and grace began to work. His merciful love cares and keeps us as the Holy Spirit forms us in our faith, with hope that our substance shall rise with Christ. I came to see how God confers nature, mercy, and grace on the sensitive soul for us to receive gifts that lead to endless life.

Assured of being in God, our sensible soul begins to sense that God is in it and he made it his City from the beginning to be his immovable seat, as God wants to dwell in the soul forever, as revelation 16 says: *Jesus comes to reside in our soul never to depart.* All gifts God gives to creatures he gives to his Son, such as dwelling in us until our soul and body mature and come to the stature ordained by nature, upon which the Holy Spirit mercifully builds, graciously inspiring gifts in us that lead to endless life.

I came to see, perceive, and understand how our soul is a created-trinity—known and loved from the beginning by the uncreated Blessed Trinity that it images, and to which it is to be united. This is sweet and marvelous to behold, assuring me of peace, rest, and delight.

God preserved our honorable body-soul unity from a double death by having the Second Person of the Trinity take our lower sensing nature (he took our higher part at creation). Christ's one soul had both higher and lower parts; the higher part was at complete peace, joy, and bliss with God; the sensible part had to suffer for man's salvation.

The 8th revelation showed this when I saw Christ's passion and death in my body and mind, having a subtle feeling and intimate inward revelation when I couldn't even look upward to heaven due to the friendly service done to me. Then I had a mighty revelation of Christ's higher part's inner life with his precious soul endlessly rejoicing in the Godhead.

Chapter LVI

God Is Closer than Our Own Soul

It is easier to know God than one's own soul. We don't come to know our soul, which is deeply rooted in God and treasured by him, until we know God, our Maker, to whom it is united. Thus the Holy Spirit kindly leads us to perfection: to know our soul well and how it is in God.

So, God is closer to us than our own soul, which is kindly founded on God's endless love that binds our substance and sense-nature strongly and inseparably together for it to stand and rest: if we know our soul by communing in alliance with it, then we'd seek our Lord God in whom it is enclosed (the 16th revelation will say more on this).

Our soul is our substance with its sense-part all united in God. Our Lord Jesus reigns in the honorable city of our sense-soul, which encloses him. While

Christ's blessed soul rest in the Godhead it encloses our substance.

We should long for this and do penance until we are so immersed in God that we truly know our own soul. In the same love and mercy that our good Lord made us and endured his blessed passion, he also leads us to this knowledge. We never fully know God until we know our own soul clearly in the light of Christ's passion as his mercy and grace rewards our tribulations, making our soul and its powers fully holy.

God's influence in the soul is founded on nature, as our reason is founded on God, from whom mercy and grace spring and is given to us, working all things that fulfills us and fill us with joy.

Nature, mercy, and grace are one in goodness and action, working all things in and for us. We should realize and seek, with all our heart, to know him and our soul more, since fully knowing God in his works is the endless joy and bliss of heaven; God wants this to begin here in knowing his love.

Knowing and loving God will only benefit our reason by founding our nature on his mercy and grace, which work for our goodness; only this can save us. In our first making, God gave us reason as a good of nature received in our spirit alone—with greater goods are to be added in his endless wisdom.

Chapter LVII

Christ Unites Our Two Natures

Christ takes the substance of all to be saved to make us noble and rich by honoring him in doing his will always. He loves that we spare nothing to truly do what pleases him: he then rewards our soul with noble virtues, knitting it to our sensing body.

Even when our sense-soul fails, our substance is full, as God's copious mercy and grace actively flow from his nature to restore us, opening us to more mercy and grace.

In God, our nature is whole; diversities flow out to fulfill his will: nature preserves us; mercy and grace restores and fills us. Our nature's higher part is imperishable as bound to God in his making us; the lower part is bound to God in Christ's incarnation, uniting our two natures. In Christ the whole Trinity is present; in Christ our higher part is rooted as our lower part was prepared for him to take. Certainly, all God's works—past, present, and future—were fully known and foreseen from the beginning, becoming man in the same Love in which he made us.

Uniting Our Sensitive Part

The next good we receive is faith, as we begin to profit from the riches of our sensitive soul arising from God's nature as his mercy and grace acts in us. God's Commandments help faith to understand how each action bids us to love him by keeping them and to know, hate, and refuse what they forbid. God also ordains the seven Sacraments and all kinds of virtues to accompany faith.

God's goodness gives us these virtues, as the Holy Spirit's mercy renews them with gifts of grace as treasures for us in Jesus Christ. In the Virgin's womb God knits himself to our body and sense-soul to become perfect man, knitting himself to each man to be saved. Christ is perfect Man. Our Lady is not only a Mother who encloses us, we are also born of her in Christ (as our Savior's Mother she is Mother of all to be saved); yet our Savior is also our Mother as we are inseparable from him in whom we are endlessly borne.

He revealed this by saying: *We are all enclosed in him and he in us,* as the 16th revelation said: *he sits in the soul.*

He is so happy to reign in our mind, to sit, rest, and dwell in our soul endlessly, as we do his will as attentive helpers, soaking in his lessons, keeping his laws, and desiring to do what he does in complete trust.

Our being is truly in God's loving and sweet affection and in truth's light and knowledge, beyond any created thing. This is not vain-glory, self-love, or some evil affection (for they just don't fit here). Only finding Jesus—not his shadow—encloses, rests, and anoints our desires; for we best find him whom we seek the more we desire him in the kind of prayer, meditation, or devotion that stirs up great and pure desires and feelings for him in us… Look at Jesus' mercy and kindness. Gently, in the recesses of your soul, ask: Where did I lose him? Sin has so blinded our soul's reason that we'd never have found him had he not preserved our reason to be able to rediscover him in our soul. He is in us yet we are not in him—as we did lose him—until we find and get closer to him. In his mercy he only let himself to be lost where he can be found: we don't need to go to Rome or Jerusalem to find him, but turn to our own soul where he is hid, as the Prophet says: *You are truly the God hidden in our soul that we may find him there*. As the Gospel says: *The kingdom of heaven is like a treasure hid in the field; when a man finds it, he joyfully goes and sells all that he has to buy that field.*

Until his image is reformed in us, Jesus remains a distant stranger. Let's form ourselves to his likeness of humility and charity, so he will know and become familiar with us, and teach us his secrets. As he tells his disciples: "He who loves me will be loved by my Father, and I will manifest myself to him." It is humility and charity, more than any other virtue or good work, that makes us like our Lord and acceptable to him. As he says: *Learn of me for I am meek and humble in heart*. He doesn't say, *learn of my going barefoot* or *my forty-day fast in the desert* or *how I chose disciples*, but of my meek humility of heart.

Of charity he says: *This is my commandment: love one another as I have loved you: by this all men will know you are my disciples*, not *do miracles, cast out demons, preach*, or *teach*, but *love one another* and, *love your neighbor as yourself*. So, if you want to be like him love humbly.

Feebly I now tell you how to penetrate to the root of our sin and truly uproot it so as to recover our soul's full dignity. Focus your thoughts, mind, and purpose on seeking and finding Jesus' presence and grace, nothing else. This is painful, as vain thoughts invade the mind and weigh down the heart hiding vestiges of his name with dark and ill-favored images of our own soul, without the light and joy of knowing and loving God. This is not Jesus' image but a body of sin and death, as St. Paul calls it. We should ignore this dark image in us. It is not real at all, as we discover when we focus on where our soul can rest, which is not on bodily things.

A dark conscience is just a lack of light and love for God. Sin is nothing, a lack of good. So, just as sin's foundation abates and dries us up, our soul is reformed into Jesus' image when our heart turns inward to find Jesus, instead of nothingness or vestiges of his name. Jesus Christ enlightens our understanding and drives out the darkness of ignorance; to love and become like him frees of tedious bitterness or heaviness.

Let's learn to let Jesus Christ into our thoughts, driving out all darkness by active prayer and fervent desires for God, focusing not on the nothingness but on whom we desire, Jesus Christ. Rise by reflecting firmly on his passion and humility. Beat down and battle, just as you do the Devil, the dark image by despising its darkness and nothingness that hides Jesus and his joy. Seeking to find only him overcomes this darkness of conscience. I describe this spiritual path to stir you to embrace it in grace. This darkness of conscience and nothingness is the image of the first Adam, as St. Paul describes: *As we have borne the image of the earthly man, the first Adam, we shall also bear the image of the heavenly man, Jesus, the second Adam.* St Paul often had to bear this heavy and cumbersome image: *O who will deliver me from this body of death*. He then comforts us: *The grace of God through Jesus Christ.*

Chapter LVIII

Life of Nature, Mercy, and Grace

The blessed Trinity is God, boundless Being, without beginning or end, with endless purpose to make mankind. The whole Trinity was in full accord to first prepare our fair nature for God's Son, the Second Person; then he made us all at once, uniting us to himself in clarity and nobility. In virtue of this precious union, God deigns that we love and seek our Creator so as to endlessly praise, thank, and enjoy him; this ongoing activity takes place in every soul to be saved. So, our almighty Creator is our nature's Father; his Wisdom is our nature's Mother in the Holy Spirit's love and goodness: they are one God, one Lord. In uniting us to himself he is our true spouse. He is pleased to say of his beloved wife and beautiful virgin: *I love you and you love me, and our love shall never be separated.*

The whole Trinity acts, as Father, Mother, and Lord in one God. Without beginning, our almighty Father creates, keeps, and rewards our nature; the Second Person's all-knowing wisdom preserves, restores, and saves our sense-soul as Mother, Brother, and Savior; our good Lord, the Holy Spirit, rewards our life and travail, endlessly surpassing all joy in his kind and copious grace.

So our life is three: in our nature we have being; in mercy we grow, and in grace we find fulfillment.

I see the Second Person as Mother of our sensing soul, for by God's making we are both substantial and sentient. In creating our being, God Almighty is Father of the higher part; in mercifully taking our nature the Second Person of the Trinity became Mother, founding our sense-part. Christ is inseparably our Mother, helping us grow as he reforms and restores us in mercy by his passion, death, and resurrection, uniting us to his substance. So he is Mother to all his children who obediently yield to him.

I understood the Trinity's might to be Father of our nature and substance; its wisdom, our Mother; and its great Love, our Lord.

Grace working with mercy pertains especially to the Third Person, the Holy Spirit as he generous outpours truth to a creature who suffers or freely does kind acts, rewarding him beyond what he deserves.

So we have our being in God, our almighty Father; our reform and restoration of all our parts in him who is perfect man, Mother of mercy; our fulfillment in the Holy Spirit's generous rewarding grace. So our substance is in our Father, almighty God; in our Mother, the all-wise God; and in our Lord, the Holy Spirit, the all-good God. Our substance is whole in the Trinity, one God, but our sense-soul is only in the Second Person, Christ Jesus, who is in the Father and the Holy Spirit. Christ's devout might leads us out of hell and earthly wretchedness to bestow on our substance his blissful heaven, abundant riches, noble virtues, and the Holy Spirit's grace and action.

Chapter LIX

Jesus Is Our Mother

God's mercy and grace bestows on us such bliss: yet we might never have bestowed it bliss had wickedness not opposed God since in conquering wickedness the goodness of mercy and grace glorifies all to be saved and makes all things good. God fights evil with the good that Jesus Christ does as our very Mother, giving us being and such sweet care of endless Love. All these revelations show how God is both our Father and our Mother, especially in the sweet words: *it is I… Fatherhood's might and goodness; it is I, Motherhood's wisdom; it is I, blessed Love's light and grace that: it is I, the Trinity, it is I, the Unity and sovereign goodness of everything. I enable you to love: I enable you to seek: it is I, the endless fulfillment of all true desires.*

The soul is highest, most noble and worthy, when it is lowest, meekest, and most humble, grounding all our sensing-nature's virtue in mercy and grace.

Our great Father, God almighty, Being itself, loves us into existence when time began. The deep charity and foreseeing counsel of the whole Trinity marvelously willed that the Second Person would become our Mother. Our Father wills, our Mother works, our good Lord, the Holy Spirit, confirms: so let's reverently love, thank, and praise our God who made our being, praying intensely to our Mother for mercy and pity, with the help and grace of the Holy Spirit, our Lord.

Our life is founded on these three: nature, mercy, and grace, making us meek and mild, with patience and pity, proper to a life of virtue that hates sin and wickedness. Jesus' Motherhood is also threefold: first, he creates our nature; he then he takes our nature to confer grace; third, he acts in our nature, distributing that grace to each; all this he does in one Love. The Second Person's Motherhood is so beautiful and noble in both in nature and grace, with a will that is godly, whole, and endlessly secure.

Chapter LX

A Kind and Loving Mother

Our Lord revealed how his Motherhood's kind love creates our nature, how it will never leave us, and how the Motherhood of mercy and grace restores our true nature.

He is our Mother by nature and grace, humbly taking our lowly flesh in the Virgin's womb (as seen in the first revelation of the Virgin's meek stature in conceiving). Our great God, sovereign Wisdom, arrayed himself in our poor, lowly flesh to serve as Mother of all things.

A mother's service is near (in nature), ready (in love), and sure (in truth). Only Jesus could truly fulfill it. He bore us in his pain and death as our good, all-loving Mother, raising us to the joy of endless life: may he be blessed as he sustains us in himself in love; at the fullness of time he suffered the sharpest travails and the most grievous pains to the end to take us to heavenly bliss, yet his love is even greater: *If I could suffer more, I would.*

He can die no more yet continues to feed us, like a good mother whose love turns her into a debtor to her child. A mother nurses her infant with her milk; our precious Jesus most kindly and tenderly does so with himself in the Blessed Sacrament, my precious food; he sustains us mercifully and graciously with all the Sacraments, as he said: *It is I that Holy Church preaches and teaches,* that is, *All the Sacraments' healing and life, all my Word's virtue and grace, all the goodness ordained in Holy Church is for you, it is I.* While a mother nurses a child tenderly at her breast, Jesus intimately nurses us to his open side to nurse us with the joys of heaven and spiritual security of endless bliss (revealed in revelation 10 when he said: *See how I love you*, as I peered into his wounded side.)

Mother is a fair and lovely word, related to the word, *nature,* which is truly proper to him who is our very Mother and mother of all. Natural love, wisdom, and knowing flow from motherhood and foster bodily health, but do little for the spirit. Yet our kind and loving Mother knows all our needs, caring for us tenderly as mothers do. As a child grows, a mother's love moves her care to adapt: she may discipline an older child to help him acquire virtues, grace, and break vices; our Lord does this beautiful work, sending us grace to the lower part to help us love in the higher part. He wants to cultivate true love for our Father, responding to God's blessed paternal and maternal love for us; as he said: *It is I whom you love.*

Chapter LXI
Spiritual Upbringing

He uses more tender care in our spiritual upbringing than in anything else, making our soul more and more precious to him as he cultivates our understanding, directs our ways, enlightens our conscience, comforts our heart, strengthens our faith, knowledge, and reverent awe of his Holy Godhead, sweet humanity, blessed passion, and surpassing goodness. So we come to love what he loves and to be pleased in him and his works. If we fall, he quickly raises us with a lovely call that draws our whole will to choose to be his servants and lovers forever.

While some fall hard and more gravely, we unwisely suppose that this is a waste; but no. For if we don't fall, we won't know how feeble and wretched we are or how marvelous is our Maker's love for us. Despite having sinned greatly, he never diminishes his love or our value in his sight and still wants us to see him in heaven. This reveals God's endless love, stronger and more marvelous than our trespasses, which he uses to help us grow in humility and meekness to reach a place in heaven, beyond what we'd reach without that meekness. So we can profit from our falls to reach the reward of God's mercy.

At times, a mother lets a child fall and be hurt a bit for its own good, but her love never allows serious peril to befall a child. If earthly mothers do this then our Jesus would never let us children perish: for he is almighty, all-wise, and all-loving—blessed be God!

Seeing our wretched falls can cause us great shame and fear so as to lose hope. But our kind Mother doesn't want this—nothing scandalizes him—but for us to become a child, running with haste and might for him to alleviate our hurt and fear. So be a meek child, saying: *Have mercy on me, oh kind and honorable Mother: I am so foul, unlike you; without your help and grace I can't become clean.*

If we ever feel uneasy, rest assured that our wise Mother sees how it may be better for a child to mourn and weep, waiting for the best time with compassionate pity and love. In health and in woe he wants us to trust like a child in his loving mother.

So in the Faith of Holy Church, let all blessed Christians encounter our honorable Mother in the solace of true understanding. Rest assured, despite feeling broken, remaining firmly and meekly united to our Mother, Holy Church, for Christ Jesus is whole and never broken. For our Savior's honorable blood is food of mercy and the precious water is plenteous to make us clean and beautiful, with blessed wounds open to heal us; our Mother's sweet, gracious hands are ready to embrace and nurse us as her children. His office is to save us.

He glories in this and longs for our sweet response of love, for our meek and firm trust, as his gracious words reveal: *I keep you secure.*

Chapter LXII

God: Nature's Father and Mother

Having seen our frailty, falls, afflictions, contempt, rejection, and all life's possible woe—our nothingness—he showed me how his blessed might, wisdom, and love so tenderly keep us in this world for his glory, saving us in solace and comfort until he spiritually lifts us up unto heaven for his glory and our eternal joy; his love never lets our time here be wasted.

God's Nature is his being and his goodness; it is God. He is nature's foundation and substance, its Father and Mother, he is Nature itself, as all created nature flow from him to achieve his end; with man's salvation nature too shall be restored and return to him through the working of grace.

He endows nature with fullness of virtue, justice, goodness, royal nobility, and piety—he so endows other creatures partially, but man, wholey. Everything in our nature is due to God and his grace, such as Holy Church—our Mother's breast—and our own soul where our Lord dwells and where faith and understanding shall blissfully find all in him.

But no one can take this honor for oneself; for our fair and noble nature belongs to our precious Christ for the glory, joy, and bliss of our salvation as he foresaw from the beginning.

Chapter LXIII

Sin, a Horrible Disease

Both nature and grace lead us to hate sin. While nature is all good and fair, grace comes to save nature by destroying sin and restoring nature's original blessedness, nobility, and honor in God by growing virtue. God's holy will beholds Nature in endless joy, purifying it in the fire of tribulation to become flawless. So nature and grace are both of God and inseparably united in one love.

When, by God's mercy and help, we live according to nature and grace, sin truly becomes more vile and painful than hell. It is unclean and unnatural, thus contrary to a beloved soul called to be all fair and shining in God's sight, as nature and grace teaches.

True dread of sin must somehow benefit us: but let's meekly moan to our honorable Mother asking him to sprinkle his precious blood on us to make our soul soft and mild, fully healing us for his glory and our endless joy. He won't delay his sweet and beautiful work until all his honorable children are born and raised (seen in his spiritual thirst and love-longing that endures until Judgment day).

So our life is founded on our true Mother, Jesus, on his all-foreseeing wisdom, the Father's great might, and the Holy Spirit's sovereign goodness. By taking our nature he gives us life; his blessed death on the Cross engenders us to eternal life; his great, sovereign, kind Motherhood feeds and nourishes us, his needy children, until Judgment day.

Our heavenly Mother is fair and sweet to our soul, gifting her gracious children with all the virtues proper to our nature, making us precious and lovely to her sight: for a child never despairs but only trusts in its mother's love, not in itself, loving its mother and each of her children as brothers and sisters, pleasing our heavenly Mother.

There is no higher peak in this life than for a feeble and powerless child to have a gracious Mother to bring it to its Father's heavenly bliss; his sweet words reflect this: *All shall be well* and *you shall see yourself all kind of things shall be well.* Then our bliss in Christ shall newly begin in the joys of our God and shall last forever.

Thus all his blessed children who come from him by nature shall return to him by grace.

Chapter LXIV

Longing for Death (Revelation 15)

Earlier I had a great desire for the gift of heavenly health and bliss to deliver me of this life and its temporal illness and woe: had I no pain in this life but the absence of our Lord, I might bear it longer. This longing made me sad. Also in my own wretched sloth and weakness I didn't want to live in travail, as I was called to do.

Then our kind Lord answered me: *Soon I will take away all your pain, illness, disease, and woe. I shall carry you up and be your reward in perfect love and bliss. Suffering and weak-will shall cease, leaving only endless joy and bliss. Can't you suffer with me a bit to glorify me?*

In these words: *Soon I will take away all your pain*, I saw how God increases our patience, rewarding us for doing his will in life. Not knowing when one will die helps, for knowing the time one might lack the patience to endure while still in the body. So God makes it seem that death is always close: our life and languish here is but a point before pain disappears and we enter bliss.

Then I saw a heavy, shapeless, and ugly body lying on the earth, like a rotting and stinking quagmire. Then from it sprang a fully formed beautiful little child—nimble, lively, and lily-white—that swiftly glided up to heaven. The foul body represented the great wretchedness of our dying flesh and the beautiful little child, our pure soul. I thought: the child shares no beauty with the body and the body shares no foulness with the child.

So it is better to remove man from pain, than pain from man; for pain may always return. Our Lord's marvelous compassion comforts a loving soul greatly in death with the promise that we shall be taken from pain and woe: *I shall carry you up and be your reward in perfect love and bliss.*

God graces us to consider this often, as such contemplation leads the soul to God and to greater glory. If spiritual and bodily heaviness, pains, or frailty blind us we know that God doesn't forgets us, as he says: *Suffering and weak-will shall cease, leaving only endless joy and bliss. Can't you suffer with me a bit to glorify me?*

Throughout our earthly stay God wants to console us in his promises, to see our pain and woe as little or nothing. If we do so for love, it will increase in value and reward.

Chapter LXV

Suffering Is Nothing

When one resolves to love God, he can be sure of being loved endlessly: God graces him with endless love and strengthens him in the hope of heavenly bliss here to make sure we get there. This hope pleases him, conferring joy on us with reverent, holy, respectful, and meek fear of our Lord as we marvel at the Lord's greatness and our own littleness. For God's beloved endlessly fosters these virtues as he sees, feels, and desires our Lord's gracious presence above all things in reverent fear, true faith, sure hope, and generous charity, granting us sweet, delectable, and marvelous assurance.

God wants love to bind me to him as if he had done it all just for me; every soul should think this and see God as its Lover. God's love creates such unity that it makes us inseparable from him.

Knowing that a friend's hand has conquered the Enemy's power completely, helping us love without dread, as a soul only reverently fears him whom he loves. All other fears pertain to the passions, bodily illness, and imaginations. So, while we suffer much pain, woe, and distress, we can treat them lightly and as nothing. Why? Because we come to know and love God with a reverent fear as our Lord gives us great peace, rest, and pleasure. As he says: *Can't you suffer with me a bit to glorify me?* God gave me these fifteen revelations, that the Spirit may renew them all in us.

Chapter LXVI

Revelations End; Pain Returns; the Devil Attacks

These revelations began early morn, about four o'clock, and came to me steadily, one after another, until just pass nine. The Lord revealed a sixteenth revelation the following night to conclude and confirm the previous ones.

I first want to share my wretched feebleness and blindness. My earlier pain, grief, and distress were taken from me during the fifteen revelations. As they ended and I sensed I would live, my sickness returned: first in my head with a loud din, then my whole body felt ill, barren, and dry as before. I moaned and cried like a wretched creature due to the pains, as if I never had any spiritual or bodily comfort.

A Religious came to ask how I fared. I said I had been delirious today. He laughed loud and heartily. Then I said I saw the cross put before my face to bleed fast. Then the Religious became all serious and marveled. Suddenly I felt ashamed at my recklessness, thinking: *This man takes seriously every word I say*. Seeing how he took it seriously, I said no more but wept for shame and wanted to go to Confession but there was no priest around and would he even believe me? I did believe during the revelation, desiring and intending to do so forever, but foolishly I let my faith in our Lord to wane. *Oh what a wretch I am! So great a sin and lack of kindness due to my folly and a little bodily pain, forgetting the comfort of our Lord's blessed appearance. See me as I truly am.*

But our kind Lord didn't leave me in this state. Trusting his mercy, I laid still until night and began to sleep. As I slept I felt the dreaded Enemy on my throat, seeing an awfully skinny and long young man, like no other I have ever seen: his face was red like freshly kilned brick, with hideous black specks. His rusty red hair was clipped in front, with locks hanging on the temples. He grinned maliciously, bearing his teeth, making him seem more horrible. He had no hands, but throttled my throat with his paws, trying to strangle me, but he couldn't.

This horrible vision came as I slept. Yet throughout I kept trusting in God's mercy and grace to save me—I barely had any life. My companions looked on me and wet my temples, comforting my heart. Suddenly smoke came in the door, with great heat and foul stench. I said: *Benedicite Domine! Everything is on fire in here!* A physical fire would have burnt us all to death, yet those with me sensed no stench, so I said: *Blessed be God!* Then I knew the Enemy had come to torment me and I remembered what our Lord had shown me that very day. I fled to the Faith of Holy Church (seeing it as my own) and found comfort. The vision vanished, and rest and peace returned without bodily illness or dread of conscience.

Chapter LXVII

Jesus Dwells in Us (Revelation 16)

Our Lord spiritually opened my eyes to see my soul: how it is a vast endless world, a holy kingdom, an honorable city where our Lord Jesus, God and Man, rests. He is fair and tall, majestically clad as a great bishop or honorable lord who devoutly rests in the soul in peace. Jesus' Godhead rules and sustains all heaven and earth, with his sovereign might, wisdom, and goodness, but comes to reside in our soul never to depart: he is pleased to dwell in this welcoming home and endless dwelling.

The Father and the Son made each creature, and the Holy Spirit, man's soul, so the whole Trinity enjoys man in endless pleasure. All creatures marvel at all the great and noble treasures and kingdoms belonging to our Lord, moving man higher, to the worthiest place where his Lord dwells. So our soul is always restless in things below or in it, but finds blissful rest beholding God his maker dwelling in him. For in man's soul is God's dwelling, and the glorious love of our Lord is the great and bright light shining in that City.

What is more enjoyable than seeing God enjoy his greatest work? If the blessed Trinity could've made man's soul any better, fairer, or nobler, his creation would be less pleasing. Let our hearts rejoice in him, rising above the earth's depths and its vain sorrows.

Chapter LXVIII

"You'll Be Conquered Not"

It pleases God and profits us to consider this delectable vision, as it makes the soul like him and his grace brings it rest and peace. To see him sitting in endless quiet and dwelling secure is a singular joy and bliss.

Our good Lord reassured me that it was truly him who revealed all this, meekly and silently saying: *I assure you that you experienced no delirium today: believe and accept it as your comfort, trusting that you'll be conquered not.*

These words confirmed my faith that he had revealed all this, beginning with how his holy passion conquers the devil, as his last words said: *You'll be conquered not.* This is God's will for all and true comfort for all my fellow Christians.

You'll be conquered not, was clear and powerful, reassuring me against any possible future tribulation. He didn't say, *Trials or afflictions you'll have not*, but:

You'll be conquered not. Let's firmly heed and trust these words, whether in health and woe. For God loves and enjoys us, and wants us to love and enjoy him with firm trust; then all will go well.

After this I saw no more.

Chapter LXIX

Christ's Passion Conquers the Enemy

The Enemy then returned to torment me with his vile, dreadful, and agonizing heat and stench. I also heard two persons simultaneous clanging bells, as if calling an important meeting, with soft, and unintelligible muttering, mouthing boisterous and mocking prayers, but without any of the devotion owed to God. I was distraught.

Our Lord graced me mightily to trust him, comforting my soul, just as I would do with any soul in travail. To keep occupied, I focused on the same crucifix that had earlier comforted me, as I spoke of Christ's passion and the Faith of Holy Church, bound myself to God with all my heart and soul. I thought: *It is a great to be occupied in the Faith, to avoid sinning and being taken by the Enemy!* Thus I felt safe from all my soul's enemies in hell.

This battle continued all night until dawn, when it suddenly left, except for the stench that lasted a bit longer; him, I scorned. This is how Christ's passion conquers the Enemy and delivers us, as he had said.

Chapter LXX

Remain Steadfast in Faith

Our good Lord showed me how the revelations would pass but his good will and grace would preserve them by faith. Instead of a sign he left me true understanding of his blessed word that powerfully bid me to believe it. May I do just that—*Blessed is he!* I do believe our Savior revealed it and that it is of the Faith: so I do believe and rejoice, bound by his final words: *Remain in your faith; faith will comfort you; so entrust yourself to faith.*

While I had just forsaken it, wretch that I am, openly saying that I had been delirious that same day, yet our Lord Jesus' mercy showed me greater fullness, in the blessed light of his precious love, in the powerful and meek words: *I assure you that you experienced no delirium today,* as if to say: *While the revelation has passed and you have no ability to keep it, experience it again so that you do keep it.* This was not just for me in my crisis but to establish faith's foundation, as he say: *take it and believe as your comfort, trusting that you'll be conquered not.*

He wants to permanently etch these words into our hearts, ever steadfast in faith in his goodness and sweet command joyfully until life's end.

Enemies within and without and spiritual blindness oppose our faith, yet our precious Lover helps us know him with true teaching and spiritual lights within and without. We must sense him wisely, receive him sweetly, and remain in him faithfully, as nothing in this life surpasses the Faith. The Lord helps us keep the faith, which is tested and strengthened by suffering and opposition without which our faith would deserve no reward, according to our Lord's teaching and my vision.

Chapter LXXI

Three Kinds of Joy

Our true happiness is our Lord's joy for his love longs to look upon us, his grace drawing us to reward our soul with greater inner and outer joy, uniting us to him and to each other in true and lasting happiness.

Our Lord gives us three kinds of joy: first, that of his passion and death that makes us joyfully happy in our sad mourning, for he is God who is love. Second is the joy of security in our lover's compassionate mercy. The third, the joy of endless bliss that awaits us. This was continuously revealed to me.

In our pain and woe, the joy of his passion and Cross, helps us bear our own cross. In our sin, the joy of compassionate mercy delivers us from our enemies. To these common joys of life he adds the joy of hoping for heavenly bliss, spuring our spiritual life to contrition, devotion, and contemplation, reaffirming our faith, hope, and charity with solace and comfort.

Chapter LXXII

Sin Versus Joy

Sin still affects creatures who don't die in it, but will share in God's endless joy.

Contraries never unite. The greatest contraries are highest bliss vs. deepest pain. The highest bliss is to have a clear vision of him in endless life: truly seeing and feeling him in all-perfect fullness of joy. So, since sin is the most contrary to God's blissful joy, as long as we meddle in it we can's see God clearly. The greater the sin, the less we can see. So sin, with its sorrow, pain, and peril of death, is a kind of hell for us. While sin can kill a holy life for a time, yet we are still alive in God's sight, as he never leaves us; yet his bliss in us is incomplete until we fully see his fair joy to which grace ordains us. Thus sin temporarily kills the blessed creature's endless life.

The more the soul longs the more it clearly sees this blissful joy by the grace of loving. For despite God dwelling in us, enclosing us in his tender love as to never leave, we continue to moan, weep, and long until we clearly see his blissful Face. For only such precious bliss is free of all pain or woe.

As we moan here below we can celebrate our Lord and Maker's nearness—he in us and we in him, his great goodness reassures us of persevering. We moan with spiritual eyes blinded and weighted down by mortal flesh and sin's darkness, obscuring our God in his blissful joy and beauty; we scarcely believe and trust in his great love or in our perseverance. So let's never stop moaning and weeping, more in spirit than in body. Our soul's desire is so great and immeasurable that no creature in heaven or on earth will stop our spiritual moaning and weeping— only God's blissful joy as he alone is our solace and comfort. Seeing his fair blissful joy will wipe away all our pain and sorrow.

God's blissful vision destroys all pain and fills the loving soul with joy and bliss, as his marvelous words reflect: *It is I, it is I: it is I in the highest, it is I in the lowest; It is I in all.*

So we know three things: our Lord God; ourselves and what we are in him by nature and grace; thirdly and meekly our sin and feebleness.

Chapter LXXIII

Two Spiritual Illnesses

Our Lord's blessed teaching had three parts: true bodily visions; locutions of words our Lord formed in my mind; finally his spiritual insights that I can only partially detail and that prompt me to say more, as God gives me grace.

God revealed how sin generally affects men and women who love God, hate sin, and want to do his will, as well as two particular kinds of illness due to our travail and trials: *impatient sloth* toward our heavy burdens, and *doubting despair or dread* (of which I shall speak later). Spiritual blindness and bodily heaviness incline us to these. God leads us to amend our lives by refusing sloth and despair just as we do other sins.

Our Lord revealed his great patience and joy in loving us in his passion. His example helps us to bear our pains gladly and wisely, which please him and profit us endlessly. We suffer pain due to ignorance of his Love. While all three Persons of the Blessed Trinity (Might, Wisdom, Love) are equal, the soul responds best to Love, which we should behold and enjoy in all things. Yet we are so blind. While some believe in God's Might and Wisdom, they stop short of trusting in his Love, which hinders God's lovers the most, according to my vision.

As we come to hate sin and embrace Holy Church's ordinances, a dread comes over us as we see ourselves in our past sins. We feel shame for our everyday sins, failed commitments or impurity, or other wretchedness, making us sad and heavy, lacking almost all comfort.

Sometimes we confuse this dreadful shame for meekness, but really it is just blind weakness. Let's despise it, as we do all sin and opposition to truth. Of all the properties of the Blessed Trinity, God wants Love's security to comfort us, making his Might and Wisdom easy for us. For God's kindness forgives us when we repent and abandon our blind heaviness and doubting dreads due to sin.

Chapter LXXIV

Holy Fear of God

There are four kinds of fear: one, fright when faced with sudden frailty, bodily illness, or other non-sinful pain. Patiently borne it is good and helps purify us. Second, the dread of bodily pain, death, and spiritual enemies that wakes us from the sleep of sin. The Holy Spirit's soft comfort is imperceptible until we experience this dread, as he moves us to contrition and to seek comfort in God's mercy. Third is a doubting-dread that tends to despair until God's grace turns the bitter doubt into sweet love. It hurts our Lord when his servants doubt his goodness. Fourth is reverent fear that is gentle and fully pleases God: the more we have it the more his sweet love conquers this fear.

Brethren, love and fear sprout from our maker's goodness and shall to the end. Nature and grace move us to love and to fear. We love God's goodness and fear his lordship and fatherhood as good servants and children.

Reverent fear and love are inseparable yet distinct, working in tandem yet with distinct properties. So he who loves also fears, though it is barely felt.

We should abandon any false dread besides reverent fear, even if under the guise of holiness. Reverent fear makes us flee to our Lord's breast quickly, with all our heart and mind, from every evil, like a child to its mother's bosom, aware of our great weakness and need, and of his everlasting goodness and blissful love. Salvation's confident embrace is in him alone. Everything contrary to this natural and true fear is either totally or partially wrong. Let's recognize the true and reject what is wrong.

The Holy Spirit graciously works this natural fear both now in this life and in heaven before our gentle, kind, and delectable God, intimately uniting us to him in kind love and gentle fear.

Let's desire our Lord God in reverent fear, meek love, and firm trust; if we do, it won't be in vain. The more we trust, the more we please and honor our Lord in whom we trust. God forbid if we ever lack reverent fear and meek love, our trust soon becomes disordered. So let's ask our Lord for a heart of reverent fear and meek love in deed, so necessary to please God.

Chapter LXXV

God's Three Longings

God can take care of all our needs, and we only need three things: love, longing, and pity. His pity keeps us in his love during times of need, while his longing draws us toward heaven in the same love. God's unquenchable thirst for mankind draws his saints to be his lively members in bliss.

I saw three kinds of longing in God—in us too—with the same virtue and end. First, he longs for us to know and love him more, as is proper and profitable; second, he longs for us to share the bliss that souls now have in heaven, free of pain; third, he longs to fill us with everlasting bliss on the Last Day not only for pain and sorrow to end for all the saved, as our Faith teaches, but also with a new bliss, ordained from the beginning, copiously filling us with God. These treasures remain hidden in himself until we are ready for them.

Fulfilling this longing is truly why he came and suffered all that he did. It is so great that all will reverently and painlessly fear God, with great wonder and awe, beyond anything ever seen or felt—even heaven's pillars shall tremble and quake—worthy of God's might: to marvel in meek joy at our Maker's greatness and our littleness.

So an experience of reverent fear—both by nature and grace—leads us on the path to a life united to God. By loving and fearing God's great goodness and might, heaven's love and reverent fear before God's face shall greatly surpass any that we have now.

Chapter LXXVI

Sin Is Hell

Our Lord also showed me how souls with true reverence and fear embrace the Holy Spirit's teaching, hating sin's vileness and horrors more than hell's pains. A soul that contemplates our Lord Jesus's fair nature fears no hell but sin. So, aware of sin, we should ceaselessly pray, earnestly sacrifice, and meekly learn to avoid blindly falling into sin, and to rise quickly if we do. For the soul's greatest pain is to turn from God.

For a peaceful soul flees the thought of another man's sin as from the pains of hell, turning to God for remedy and help. For another's sin is like a thick mist that temporarily prevents us from seeing God's beauty, unless we are contrite, with a compassion for the sinner that desires God for him. Otherwise it harms and hinders us, as the revelation on compassion showed.

In this vision our Lord had revealed to me two opposites, wisdom and folly: a wise man does the will and counsel of his sovereign friend, Jesus, always united to him intimately, whether in a foul or clean state, in sickness or in health, never flee from his love. Because we change we can fall into sin, which produces doubting dread prompted by the enemy and our own blind folly. We say: *See what a wretched and unfaithful sinner I am? I don't keep his commands, I promise to do better but I fall again into sloth and wasting time* (this is where sin begins for those called to serve, according to my vision). This makes us dread to appear before our kind Lord. The enemy tries to control us with this false dread, threatening pain, weighing us down and making so weary as to distract us from turning to our fair and everlasting Friend.

Chapter LXXVII

Countering the Enemy

Our good Lord showed me how the Fiend tries to rob us of love and peace. When we fall due to feebleness and folly, the Holy Spirit's mercy and grace comes to raise us to even greater joy. If the enemy ensnares us into falling (to his pleasure) he loses much more when charity and meekness raises us. He hates our soul so much that our glorious rising causes him greater pain and sorrow, festering ongoing envy for all the sorrows he failed to inflict on us. This is why our Lord scorns him, making me laugh mightily.

Our remedy, then, is to flee to our Lord when we see our wretchedness: the needier we are the more we profit. So it is good to think: *I know my pain and punishment are great, yet my all-wise and all-good God will tenderly punish me with discreet love*. Seeing this and abiding in him with meek love, the Holy Spirit's mercy and grace urges the sinful soul to go willingly and gladly to the scourging and chastening that our Lord gives, making it tender and easy; our only satisfaction is in him and in his works.

The revelations said little of voluntary penance; in the thirteenth, God did reveal the lovely way he gives us penance to endure by meekly focusing us on his blessed passion (as friends who witnessed it were united to him in pity and love). He tells us: *Don't blame yourself too much, as though your tribulation and woe were all your fault; I don't want you to be overly down and sad. Look, no matter what you do you'll have woe. Any penance is for your benefit.*

Life on earth is a prison, a penance. God wants us to rejoice in our Lord as our remedy. He leads us to the fullness of joy. There our Lord will be our endless bliss; here he is our keeper. True love and sure trust is our way and our heaven, as the revelations led me to understand, especially the one where I chose him for my heaven (see ch. 19).

Our Lord is our comfort; we touch him and he cleanses us; we trust him and he safeguards us from all peril.

Our kind Lord makes our heart and soul at home with him, but not with reckless familiarity, as our Lord's friendship is sovereign kindness, kindness itself. Called to be endlessly with our Lord in heaven, we must imitate him in all things perfectly: this is our salvation and bliss.

If we don't know how to please and glorify our Lord as he desires, he will teach us. O bless the Lord!

Chapter LXXVIII

Contrite Awareness of Sin

Our Lord shines his kind, merciful light on our sins and feebleness, exposing their vileness and horror so that we learn four things: that he is the basis of all our life and being; second, that his powerful mercy helps us conquer our enemies when we sin and fall, even after giving them extra chances to imperil us, oblivious to our own needs (see ch. 39); thirdly, he kindly he helps us see when we go astray; fourth, he steadfastly and unchangingly abides with us, seeking our loving return and union with him and he with us.

With this gracious knowledge we can see our sins profitably without despair. We must see and feel our shame to overcome any pride or presumption: the more our Lord shows us our sins the more we realize how sinful and wretched we are. Yet he kindly limits what we see, too vile and horrible for us to endure as we are. So our blessed Savior gently heals us with contrition and grace, detaching us from all that is not his perfectly uniting us to himself.

This refers to man in general. The higher and nearer to God a soul is the more sinful it sees itself—and how I, the least and lowest, need this to be saved. Our Lord comforts me by uniting me to himself in charity; yet he still lets me sin.

Seeing him brought joy, yet I found it hard to accept this, so our kind Lord waited until his grace readied me to continue. I learned that, despite the special gift to reach heights of contemplation, we still need to see our sins and know our feebleness to acquire the meekness needed to be saved.

We cannot know this on our own or from enemies who seek our eternal undoing, so let's thank God for lovingly showing it to us in his mercy and grace.

Chapter LXXIX
Why God Lets Us Sin

He then enlightened me on why he lets us sin. As I was alone at the time I first thought it just referred to me. But our Lord graciously comforted me, revealing how it applies to all, as all of us do and will sin until the last day. As part of mankind, I hope in God's mercy, which is sufficient for us all. God only shows me my sin, and those of others, so as to comfort me or to aid my fellow Christian.

Aware of my sins helped me dread self-reliance: not knowing how I may fall or how great my sin will be.

As our kind Lord revealed his endless and unchanging love, I could rely with certainty and might on his great goodness and grace to keep our soul inseparably united to him (see cc. 37, 40, 47, 61, 82).

Such meek fear saves us from presumption and despair as his blessed revelations of Love brings us true comfort and joy. Our kind Lord's gracious revelations and teachings comfort our soul, drawing us to know the sweetness of loving him intimately. All we see or feel, within or without, that is contrary to this intimacy must be of the enemy and not of God. So, if we are lax in exercising or guarding our hearts by falsely presuming his generous love, we must react to this odious attitude contrary to God's will.

When we fall, by frailty or blindness, our kind Lord will move us to see our wretchedness, calling us to meekness. He doesn't want us to stagnate or to obsess about accusing ourselves, or to despair, but to turn to him. For alone he waits our sorrowful moaning until we return to him who comes quickly, for we are his joy and delight, and he, our life and salvation.

Alone he waits, not looking at the blessed company of heaven but at his work on earth pursuing the lost sheep, as he revealed it to me.

Chapter LXXX

Penance: Longing for Christ, Our Reward

In man's life, three things glorify the triune God that also uplift, preserve, and save man: our use of natural reason; second, the Holy Church's common teaching; third, the Holy Spirit's inward working. God confers all these, enlightening our natural reason to the Holy Church's teaching and to the Holy Spirit, with his various gifts that we should honor and cultivate. Together these three work great things in us, like knowing the *ABCs.,* the basics for reaching the fullness of heaven.

Our Faith teaches that only the Son of God took our nature, doing all the work of our salvation to bring us to our last end. He dwells in, rules, and governs us in this life to bring us to his bliss. He does this while a soul destined for heaven is still on earth as if it were the only such soul Christ brings to his bliss. I know and believe in the angels' service, as we are taught, but this was not revealed to me here. He is the nearest and meekest, the highest and lowest, he does all: all honorable things we need he does for our joy in heaven.

He *waits moaning sorrowfully* while we lack true contrition, sorrow, and compassion, not being united to our Lord: only Christ in us is beneficial. While some rarely feel this, Christ remains *morning sorrowfully* until he can bring us out of all our woe. Suffering love is never without pity. So when we stop thinking of him or guarding our soul, we fall into sin leaving Christ alone to wait *moaning sorrowfully*.

In kind reverence let's go quickly to accompany our Lord. He is here alone with us and for us. Sin, despair, and sloth estrange us from him, our Lord still waits alone for us. So, even if we sin often, it is good for us to go to him as his Goodness never leaves us alone; he remains, tenderly excusing and deflecting blame in his sight from us.

Chapter LXXXI

Dwelling with Us

In various ways our Lord is in heaven and on earth, but the only place I saw him dwell was in man's soul.

I saw his blessed Incarnation and passion on earth, and his pilgrimage here with us, leading us to heaven's bliss with him; I also saw God in a point (ch. 11). Especially he revealed how he reigns by taking his seat in man's soul to rest in his honorable city, never to be moved.

Our Lord dwells in a marvelous and stately place, ready for us to respond to his gentle touch, to rejoice in his love rather than to cry over our frequent falls. For he glories most when we lovingly bear our penance gladly as he tenderly embraces our doing penance. On earth, life is penance, as is nature's continual longing for him; his love, wisdom, and truth makes us long for him. He mercifully helps us bear our suffering for him who suffered for us. Our penance never goes away until he becomes our reward. So he wants us to set our hearts on passing over the pain we now feel to the bliss for which we hope.

Chapter LXXXII
Seeing God and Ourselves

Our kind Lord also reveals the soul's moaning sadness: *I know you live for my love, joyfully and gladly enduring the penance that comes to you; but to the extent you sin you will suffer woe, tribulation, and distress for my love all that might come. So don't let falling into sin overly grieve you.*

This shows how our Lord sees us with pity, not blame (ch. 51). While we feel guilt for sin in this passing life, his endless love gently moves us to mourn our frequent sins with restraint: that our sorrow reflects trust in his mercy, takes him as our medicine while cleaving to his love and goodness in perceiving our nothingness. In this meekness we come to see our sin by faithfully experiencing his everlasting love; to thank, praise, and please him—*I love you and you love me, our love is inseparable, making my suffering profitable.* This spiritual insight arose from the words: *I keep you secure.*

Our blessed Lord greatly desires us to live in this way, to seek, enjoy, and learn all his lessons by the gracious light of his love; what contradicts them can only be of the enemy. None of his lovers on earth can avoid falling completely: as we fall and rise we are preciously kept in one Love. We fall when we look at ourselves, and we don't when we look at God and remain faithful. Seeing our Lord is the highest truth that binds us tightly to him who teaches us his great fidelity. It is good for us in this life to see this: the higher gives us spiritual solace and true joy in God and the lower gives us holy fear and shame. But our good Lord draws us ever higher while not eliminating the lower until we come to have our Lord Jesus as our reward in the fullness of endless joy and bliss.

Chapter LXXXIII
Life, Love, and Light

In all his revelations, I sensed, saw, and felt God's three properties (life, love, and light, see cc. 85 and 86) but most clearly in the Twelfth, when he said: *It is I.* His Life is marvelous intimacy, his Love, gentle kindness, and his Light, endless beauty. These properties were one, to which I united my reason in complete trust.

With reverent fear I marveled at the vision and felt our reason's sweet accord with God. This is his greatest gift to our nature.

Our faith is a light of the endless Day to our nature; the light is our Father, God, that leads us to our Mother, Christ, and our good Lord, the Holy Spirit. He metes out this light discreetly, shining on us in our night of pain and woe, where we earn God's merit and thanks. We firmly know and believe our life's light and source, to whom we go wisely and mightily in his mercy and grace.

Then our woe ends as our God and Maker—with the Holy Spirit, in Christ Jesus our Savior—opens our eyes to see light's fullness clearly.

Our faith in God, our endless Day, is night's light.

Chapter LXXXIV

The Light Is Charity

Charity is the light that God's wisdom metes out to our profit. For the light of our blissful Day is not too bright to blind us, nor too weak, but is perfect to live well, with travail to earn God's endless praise. I saw this in revelation six when he said: *I thank you for your travail.* So, charity keeps us in faith and hope that leads to the end of all: charity.

This light of charity is three: uncreated Charity, which is God; second, created charity is our soul in God; third, the virtue of charity. Charity is a precious gift by which we love God for himself, ourselves in God, and what he loves for him.

Chapter LXXXV

Bless the Lord

I marveled at how our life here is simple yet blind, our kind Lord rejoices as this light works in us; our faith in him please him most, to endlessly enjoy him in God's bliss, praising and thanking him as he foresaw, knew, and loved us in his designs without beginning or end. His uncreated love made us; that same love safeguards us from anything that may take away our bliss. At the Judgment we shall be lifted up to see clearly the mysteries now hid. No one will say: *Lord, it would have been better had things been different*; but all will say with one voice: *Bless the Lord, for all is well! Now we see why everything was done as it was ordained before anything was made.*

Chapter LXXXVI

Our Lord Means Love

This book begun by God's gift and grace, yet it still feels unfinished.

With God's help, we pray in charity—to thank, trust, and praise—to our good Lord who said: *I am the foundation of your prayer*. Truly our Lord teaches us how he will grace us to love and trust him. For he looks on his heavenly treasure on earth with love so great that his light and solace of heavenly joy overcome any sorrow and darkness we are in, drawing our hearts to him.

Often I have longed for the full meaning of our Lord's revelations; fifteen years later I received a spiritual light: *You want to learn the meaning of all this? Learn it well: Love is its meaning. Who showed it to you? Love… Why? For Love… So hold on to what you learn to know it more. You learn or know nothing except that Love was our Lord's meaning.* So *Love* is our Lord's meaning.

God loved us before he made us he, and he never lessens that love, and never will. All his works he does and makes to profit us in this love. In this love our life is everlasting. We begin in his love and for his love he made us in him without beginning. We shall endlessly see all this in God.